This
Scarb
Meetir

CW01498685

RELATIVE EXPERIENCE

a contemporary anthology
of Quaker family life

collected and edited by

KEITH REDFERN and SUE COLLINS

QUAKER HOME SERVICE

First published June 1994
by Quaker Home Service

All rights reserved. No part of this book may be reproduced or utilised, in any form or by any means, electronic or mechanical, without permission in writing from the Publisher. Inquiries should be addressed to: The Literature Secretary, Quaker Home Service, Friends House, Euston Road, London NW1 2BY, U.K.

© QUAKER HOME SERVICE 1994

illustrations by Tim Redfern
cover design by David Goddard

ISBN: 0 85245 252 7

Printed in Great Britain by Ipswich Book Co. Ltd., Ipswich, Suffolk

CONTENTS

ACKNOWLEDGEMENTS

The editors are grateful for the permission to reproduce the following:

'Creating Mothers' from *Quaker Monthly*, May 1988.
Extracts from 'The Child' by Gujubhai; English translation by Satish Kumar first appeared in *Resurgence*.
'Two Mothers' from *Quaker Life*, April 1985.
'A Gentle Quaker Lesson' from *Quaker Life*, March 1983.
'Extracts from Grandmother's Petting Parties' from *Friends Journal*, May 1986.
'Family Confrontation' from *Quaker Life*, November 1985.
Extracts from 'Roots of Peacemaking in the Family' from *Mothering Magazine*, volume 33.
Extracts from 'Living Together, Learning Together' from *Friends Journal*, April 1985.
Extracts from 'Coming to Terms with Folk-Tale Truths' from *The Friend*, November 1979.
Extracts from 'A Welcome Letter' from *Friendly Woman*, volume 8 no: 4.
'Forcing Children to Meeting' from *Friends Journal*, June 1985.

Introduction

Although some of the writings included in this collection have been abridged. In every other respect everything is in its original form so as to represent accurately both the views and the experiences of the contributors

KEITH REDFERN and SUE COLLINS
October 1991

Foreword

The working title of this collection was *A Parenting Miscellany*, and I know that there will be those who rail at the use of the very word parenting itself. John Punshon was recently quoted as saying that 'parenting' tends to put the emphasis on the angst of the bringing up rather than the welfare of the brought up. He prefers the 'upbringing of children' to 'parenting skills'. Many would agree, but it is certainly true that some cope more easily with the raising and nurturing of their children than others, so why is this? Are there skills which can be learned, or is there only experience?

No-one can say that bringing up children is ever easy. Parents are employed in the position of ultimate responsibility but, in preparation for it, there is no training, there are no qualifications other than those biological, the working hours can seem endless and any rewards can be measured in levels of frustration, exhilaration, stress, wonder, fright and, ultimately, love.

Between them parents have an accumulated wealth of knowledge and experience which is not generally available to others seeking help or advice. Sue and I have collected previously published writings which share lessons learned or particular aspects of parenting. We have also asked and encouraged Friends to express some of this 'family hindsight' in order that others may have the opportunity to benefit from it as they both consider parenthood and learn to face and cope with some of the situations that it can bring.

What is a vocation for some can be an endurance test for others. It is not possible to be taught how to be a parent for there is no time to learn. Situations only seem to arise when they are least expected and one is not always able to phone a friend for an instant panacea or look up remedies in some sort of fail-safe manual. Parents are required to provide immediate solutions to their children's problems - relief in the direst emergency - a bump on the head; the death of a pet; homework; my boyfriend doesn't love me anymore.

It is never possible to prevent crises from arising although the development of sound and stable family relationships can make it easier to cope when anything does happen and our only previous experience may have been our observation of our own parents.

Reading these pages can give the impression that a majority of family situations are happy and successful but this is not necessarily a true reflection of reality. Many of the memories and experiences in this collection come from families in which there appear to have been no problems; contented childhoods and stable relationships. But it cannot be said of any family that nothing ever went wrong.

Some parents, in the middle of a difficult family situation and wishing to share their problem, have tried to describe their experiences. They have found it hard, in some cases impossible, to write openly for fear of exacerbating their own family crises. The offer of anonymity has not helped as hiding true identities can give writers a feeling that they are being dishonest and some Friends have not felt able to do this.

Some accounts are sad and quite harrowing. What happens when the truly unexpected happens, when tragedy strikes or everything seems to be falling apart?

And what is so special about a Quaker parent? In what way is our approach to our children, as Friends, likely to be different from that of others?

This collection is designed to help those who may be at the stage of considering starting a family, for those who face problems or despair and may get solace from discovering that they are not alone in the situation in which they find themselves. It has happened to someone else before, and they coped.

I also hope that there may be material here to assist those who are faced with providing the kind of comfort and support that parents may often need although they may not always feel able to ask for it.

The extracts from the Bible, William Penn and the Indian poet Gijubhai may seem out of place in a contemporary Quaker collection but they stand as a reminder of the variety of relationships that exist and have existed between parents and children. We have our own conception of how that relationship should be. Others may disagree.

There are no chapters in this book but an index is provided at the end to allow for easy reference to particular types of situations.

We are grateful to all who have contributed in any way to this collection and to those who have given their permission for previously published work to be included

Is there a perfect parent?   Ask the child.
Is there a perfect child?

Don't expect an objective answer from the parent but, perhaps, wait and see what kind of parent the child eventually makes.

KEITH REDFERN

PARENTING is a long dark tunnel, full of feeding, washing, teaching and being a taxi-service and, most of all, worry. But when you finally reach the daylight at the other end, and find with you an intelligent, happy adult friend, you realise what a privilege it is.

ANGELA PERRETT GREEN

Creating Mothers

When the good Lord was creating mothers he was into his sixth day of overtime when an angel appeared and said, 'You're doing a lot of fiddling around on this one.' And the Lord said, 'Have you read the specifications on this order? She has to be completely washable but not plastic...have 180 movable parts, all replaceable... run on black coffee and left overs... have a lap that disappears when she stands up...a kiss that can cure anything from a broken leg to a disappointed love affair and six pairs of hands.'

The angel shook her head slowly and said, 'Six pairs of hands? No way.'

'It's not the hands that are causing me problems.' said the Lord, 'it's the three pairs of eyes that mothers have to have.'

'That's the standard model?' asked the angel.

The Lord nodded, 'One pair that sees through closed doors when she asks, "What are the children doing in there?" when she already knows.'

'Another in the back of her head that sees what she shouldn't but what she has to know. And, of course, the ones in front that can look at a child when he gets himself into trouble and say, "I understand and love you" without so much as uttering a word.'

'Lord,' said the angel, touching his sleeve gently, 'go to bed, Tomorrow is another...'

'I can't,' said the Lord. 'I'm so close now. Already I have one that heals herself when she is sick, can feed a family of six off one pound of mince and can get a nine year old to have a bath.'

The angel circled the model very slowly.

'It's too soft', she sighed.

'But tough,' said the Lord, excitedly, 'You cannot imagine what this mother can do or endure.'

'Can it think?'

'Not only think but it can reason,' said the Lord.

Finally the angel bent over and ran her finger across the cheek.

'There's a leak,' said the angel.
'It's a tear.'
'What's it for?'
'It's for joy, sadness, disappointment, pain, loneliness and pride.'
'You are a genius,' said the angel.
The Lord looked sombre. 'I didn't put it there.'

MARIE HOLT

first published in *Quaker Monthly*: May, 1988

A Mother to Her Child

I would sing songs for you -
Make music to fill all your silences,
Paint glowing pictures, colouring dark spaces,
And for your warmth,
Light candles and bright fires,
Grow scented roses for your winter days,
Remove all thorns, smooth the rough places,
Help you to attain your dearest dreams,
And give you all the joy your heart desires,
But, all this would not bring you happiness,
This life is yours, I must not live it for you,
Or ease the pricks and blows - over-protecting.
You must explore, experience the sweetness and the sad,
And, should you need me - I shall be here - waiting.

CHRISTINE

My First Child

When my first child was born she was a great joy. She was perfectly formed, even pretty and as I looked at her I knew she was as yet unmarked by the pains and scars of experience. She was unformed in character and I had an overwhelming desire to protect her from the hurts that life would bring.

At that time I was a Roman Catholic and following tradition after the birth of a child I went to be churched. I was shocked so deeply by that service I was unable to practise any formal religion for a very long time and it left me in a state of limbo spiritually.

To look at that miracle of a baby and say she was black-stained and dirtily contaminated with original sin was something I could not tolerate.

Her perfect innocence could only be marred by human behaviour, greed, spitefulness and pettiness. Good human qualities of love, forbearance and what the Spanish call *sympatico* were there to be developed.

ANONYMOUS

Respect the child so that we can keep our self respect
Avoid shouting at a child so that we can rid ourselves
of the bad habit of shouting.
Refrain from beating a child so that we can be free
from violence and misconduct.
When we have reformed ourselves the child will
naturally grow in goodness.

from 'The Child' by Gijubhai

A Baby's Point of View

Our first baby, a daughter named Rhian, was born on Christmas Eve 1989. She is now one and the wonderful thing she has taught me is answering 'that of God in everyone.' Rhian expects to see God, and so she does. She has not learned to fear people, to worry about what they may think of her, to be prejudiced or pre-judge their thoughts or actions. Thus she makes friends of everyone she meets and truly finds and answers God. It seems such a pity that she will lose this capacity to be so receptive. I think we can learn much from watching the openness with which young children embrace the world.

CATHARINE PERRY

Where shall I play?
Where shall I jump?
To whom shall I talk?
When I talk my mummy feels interrupted.
When I play my daddy is irritated.
When I jump I am told to sit down.
When I sing I am told to be quiet.
Tell me, where shall I go, what shall I do?

from 'The Child' by Gijubhai

A Credo

I believe,

- that children were given to us to be enjoyed
- that all children, including babies, can be seen to be rational and reasonable beings, if only we strive to understand their point of view.
- that from time to time this imperfect world will deny to children their heart's desires. If we must be the instrument of this denial, let it be because life has made it so, not because the denial satisfies our own values, tastes and convenience.
- that children at all ages know us better than we believe. Nature has endowed them with the power to understand the messages we give them from our actions, our attitudes and the spaces between the words.

Being shaped by these messages, for good or ill, is known as 'growing up.'

WILL FARRIER

Two Mothers

A woman sat by the hearthside place
Reading a book, with a pleasant face
Till a child came up, with a childish frown
And pushed the book, saying 'Put it down.'
Then the mother, slapping his curly head,
Said, 'Troublesome child, go off to bed;
A great deal of Christ's life I must know
To train you up as a child should go.'
And the child went off to bed to cry,
And denounced religion by and by.
Another woman bent over a book,
With a smile of joy and an intent look,
Till a child came up and jogged her knee
And said of the book, 'Put it down - take me.'
Then the mother sighed as she stroked his head,
Saying softly, 'I never shall get it read;
But I'll try by loving to learn his will,
And his love into my child instil.'
That child went to bed without a sigh,
And will love religion by and by.

ANONYMOUS
first published in *Quaker Life* April 1985

A Gentle Quaker Lesson

During the four years that I was the youngest in our Quaker
household I made it my privilege to spoon from the berry bowl
the biggest strawberries or the juiciest peace slices. From the
cookie plate, I selected the one with most sugar on top.

One evening at supper, my father said, 'We are going to
play a game.'

'Goody,' I said, and wondered if my dignified parent was
suggesting 'Mother, May I?' or 'Stairstep School' for after-
supper fun.

'We will play the game right here at the table,' my father said. 'First, pick up the serving spoon.' Obediently, I did this. 'Now close your eyes.' Since I could not think of a way to peek, I closed my eyes tightly.

'Dip into the berry bowl and lift the spoon... Good. Now open your eyes and put on your plate whatever the spoon has on it.'

When cookie selection time came, we played the game for the second time. My father said, 'Close your eyes again. Put your finger down easily... Open your eyes and take the one you touched.'

Thus I began learning the larger lesson of accepting with grace whatever life 'dishes out'.

KARLA MINEAR
first published in *Quaker Life*, March 1983

Extracts from
Grandmother's Petting Parties

One of the big treats of my early life was to spend a couple of weeks each summer in the great rambling Jacobs house with its huge attic full of ancient treasures.

Grandmother was always baking - cherry and apple pies with incredibly tender crisp crusts, cinnamon rolls, loaves of white and whole wheat bread.

She would let me roll out the crusts and make a tiny pie of my own, baked in its own miniature tin.

When all the baking was safely in the oven, grandmother would take me into the living room and seat herself in her sturdy rocking chair. She would smile, stretch out her arms and say, "Come here, Vernie boy, let's have a petting party." She took me into her lap and hugged me tight against her generous bosom while she rocked and hummed her favourite hymns. She would speak softly into my ear, telling me how special I was, how much she loved me, and how proud she was of me. She rocked and rocked and rocked, while a kind of cosmic peace seeped through all my bones and sinews and mind and heart and soul.

Ever since that time I have had no difficulty believing that there is a personal mind and loving purpose behind the universe. And I have found it quite impossible to believe in any eternal hell of punishment. The One behind this creation is at least as loving as my grandmother; no doubt about it.

VERN ROSSMAN
first published in *Friends Journal* 15.5.86

Adult Education

In almost every country there is a system of compulsory education. The most important educational process that children take part in is the education of their parents. Unfortunately, before they can begin to educate them, the infant has an even more important task that he must perform. He must carefully choose the right parents. I have spent many years dealing with what have been called 'problem children'. In almost every case the problem has been caused by the children choosing the wrong parents in the first place. However, having made their choice, it is the duty of the child to educate them as well as possible.

For the baby, the task is simple. Many parents, especially fathers, have a strange idea about babies. They think that they need to work out what babies and toddlers should eat, when they should sleep, what they should play with and when they can be ignored. They imagine that the little one will be glad to carry on according to this formula. The little one concerned will spare no effort - to the point of total exhaustion - in dispelling these illusions. A father may believe, for example, that he can make a little girl eat what he thinks is good for her. In the real world, in a contest between a grown man with a spoon and a baby with a will of her own, there can be only one winner. Father soon learns that he can make the baby sick, he cannot make her eat.

To drive home the lessons, babies have several powerful teaching aids. There is the throwing up (which babies enjoy). There is also the terrifying high temperature, combined with the purple face. My own children, as babies, could effortlessly bring on a high temperature, at a moment's notice, for any suitable occasion.

I must mention one other instrument of persuasion. I well remember my little daughter, whom I met for the first time on leaving the army at the end of the war. We went on the Woolwich Ferry. She liked it so much that she didn't want to leave. My wife said, 'Let me talk to her.' I said that this was a time to learn proper behaviour. I was right. It was a time for learning and my little girl was ready to teach me. I picked her up and carried her away. Her crying filled the ship. Her cries filled the High Street and woke the borough of Woolwich. She screamed for the whole tramway journey home. In my arms her screams deafened me and when I put her down she lay stretched on the paving stones and screamed even louder. Doors opened all the way down the street. I learned that the voice of a little girl is stronger than the arms of the strongest man.

We grown-ups may feel that they don't have to teach us with such brutality, but every child knows that the good teacher is severe at first so that he can learn to love the pupils later on.

When the toddlers become girls and boys they teach us that they can play in the rain without getting wet, that at night time the floor is the proper place for clothes and that peace and quiet is harmful to the human spirit.

Later, when they are youngsters, one learns that it is pointless to ask, to try to discover or to worry about where they are going, what they are doing or whom they are doing it with. Any conversation on this theme will run something like this.

'Where are you going?'

'Out.'

'Out where?'

'Just out.'

'And what are you going to do, "Just out"?'
'Nothing.'
'And who are you going to do nothing with?'
'Nobody.'
'Any particular nobody?'
'Nobody. Anybody. I don't know.'
'Do we know them?'
'Perhaps, I don't know.' And so on.

If the parents learn these simple lessons they will grow up sane, healthy and, within reason, happy. If they fail to learn they will suffer headaches, ulcers and a disposition to talk about how things were different when they were children.

In the end, perhaps the most valuable thing that parents can do for their children is to offer them a model of properly behaved parenthood. Otherwise the children may also grow up to be uneducated, badly behaved parents. Nations who do not learn the lessons of history are condemned to live their history again. It is the same with families.

WILL FARRIER

The child will eat don't feed her
The child will bath don't force him.
The child will walk don't push her.
The child will sing don't make him sing.
The child will play don't interfere.
The child wants to be self reliant.

from 'The Child' by Gijubhai

Family Confrontation

A church sign board I recently saw stated; 'A closed mouth gathers no feet!' At times this can be a healthy solution to many family problems. However, what is said isn't as big a problem as the way it is said.

It seems one of the hardest tasks the family faces today is that of confrontation. How does a parent handle a child when the child is doing something the parent feels is wrong? How does a child confront parents when the child feels an injustice is done?

It seems that sometimes 'speaking the truth' can be very hazardous to one's health. All of us at sometime in our lives have been hurt by those who felt it was their duty to 'tell it like it is!' Although honesty is necessary for good communication, how we speak the truth can make all the difference.

In the Bible, we find an important Scripture that directs us in this matter. In *Ephesians* 4:15, Paul says, 'Speak the truth in love.' This means the truth can and should be communicated in loving ways. Let us look at some ways we may be able to do this:

1) First of all what we say in truth is very important. Some statements can automatically send up 'red flags'. Red flags are verbal signals, not unlike the signals given to the bull to charge. An example of such verbal red flags can be found in 'you' statements. If one is not cautious 'you' statements quickly tend to attack self-worth/respect. Some examples are:

> 'You must be pretty ungrateful and irresponsible because you didn't clean up your room!'

or

> 'You are mean and inconsiderate for yelling at me in front of my friends.'

The nature of love is to build one another up, not destroy. A more loving and honest way to communicate is with 'I' statements. Examples of 'I' statements could be:

'I feel like I have failed as a parent when I walk into your room. Is there some way we can work on a system of keeping it clean?'

or

'I really feel embarrassed when I am corrected in front of my friends. From now on could we talk about problems in private or when my friends leave?'

2) Another important issue in confronting members of your family is timing. When you do it can be crucial. When the moving van pulls away from the home of your child's best friend. It isn't a good time to remind him of his friend's bad qualities! Neither are remarks about your mother's cooking appropriate while she is pulling a burnt roast out of the oven.

Although I am not sure we can ever be certain the time is right to confront lovingly, we can and must be sensitive to when the time is wrong and no love will be felt.

3) Finally, how you say the truth in love is essential. One's tone of voice can make a difference in whether truth is accepted in love or not. No matter what the words are, if one detects resentment, anger, etc... it is those feelings that are going to be communicated. In all probability neither yelling nor whining will convey the truth you need to communicate in love.

The family environment is the ideal place where we can learn to confront. Yet the model for confrontation must always be neutralized by love.

JUDY DENNIS
first published in *Quaker Life,* November 1985

Whether there is nectar or poison in our eyes,
Whether our speech is sweet or bitter,
Whether our touch is soft or harsh,
Whether our mind is respectful or disdaining,
The child senses it immediately,
The child knows it all.

from 'The Child' by Gijubhai

A few years ago I wanted to begin to change the focus of my peacework. I had been like many others, active in the peace movement. Apart from the usual campaigning activities I had also been working with groups within the movement on issues of Taking Heart in the Nuclear Age, Conflict Resolution and suchlike. A recurring theme which surfaced in the work was the issues of relationships - how we relate to others and the world around us, how we relate to that of God in others and ourselves, and how the way we relate now is affected by the first experiences we had of relating. Often these experiences were not good enough to help us deal with life as it presents itself to us today - and this through no fault of our own.

Since 1945 (the bomb) children are brought up by parenting people who can no longer act from the inner certainty that there will be a future. Over the years we have begun to allow this knowing into our consciousness. The connection between this knowledge on the one hand, and our insights about wholeness and the experience we bring from our own wounded learning on the other hand is the new framework in which we have to learn anew and to teach how to build enhancing relationships, especially with regard to our children.

Most people enter into parenthood without knowing much about raising children, yet it is in the family (of whoever the family consists) that children learn to build relationships. Often we see therefore a repetition of patterns developing which result in unsuccessful relationships between parents/ adults and children which could have been helped or might have been prevented by a better understanding about the expectations around parenthood, parents' needs and the effect of one's own experiences.

When I am writing this we are at war - humanity is fighting humanity - we are fighting ourselves. What does this have to say about how we relate and learned to relate - isn't what happens in our own family life a mirror of what happens in the family of nations and vice versa? Can we begin to apply the lessons we are learning from our own families (in family therapy, counselling, etc.) to the global family? This is about getting to grips with the meaning of 'we are all interconnected - part of each other and the creation around us'. What I do to/ for the environment I do to/for myself. What I do to/for myself I do to/for others: the effect of what I do does not just apply to me alone.

To come back to parenting - one of the deeper meanings of this war, it feels to me, is for us as Quaker parents an invitation to incorporate the Peace Testimony into our parenting here and now. Conflicts and disagreements can be used creatively. We can look at them as invitations to grow and discover our own and others' potential; our diversity (created as we are in the image of God) as a possibility for rejoicing rather than as reason for destroying each other. This takes time. In the family, at school, at work. Time to listen and learn listening skills, a will to use new ways of relating of which mediation and conflict resolution are only two.

We can re-examine our view of children: how far is it affected by what we experienced as a child ourselves? What needs to be healed for the child in me? Am I really helping my child to become an independent responsible adult by solving all her/his problems? Or is this about my own sense of security?

Parents can come together and share experiences and new skills such as happens in the Parent Network programme called Parent Link*. Parents can also offer each other support in bringing up children - it is in particular single parents who often miss out on this.

Learning to relate begins as a child. What we learned then affects all our adult relating. When we fully understand this we are holding one of the keys to building peace. And hopefully this understanding will also contribute to our valuing parenthood for what it is: the most important job people can do.

MARIA BROWN

* *The Parent Network*, 44-46 Caversham Road, London NW5 2DS.

Extracts from
Roots of Peacemaking in the Family

I do not know any parent, especially those active in nuclear disarmament efforts, who wish to expose his or her young children to information that details the grotesque scenario of a nuclear holocaust. Even for many adults, it is too much to focus on, and we often allow ourselves to bury the thought by immersing ourselves in the busyness of our daily lives, at the same time trying to appease our guilt feelings about doing little or nothing to help prevent such a holocaust.

But isn't such an attitude both unfortunate and unnecessary? I believe there are two ways to immerse oneself in the daily tasks of parenting and making a living. One is to refuse to look at the suffering and darkness in the world (including that in our own hearts) and to use busyness as a curtain of unwillingness to see. Following this way seems to me not to protect our children but to rob them of the real possibilities of learning how to foster peace, both inner and outer.

The second way is to recognise and take into one's heart and consciousness the suffering and dangers mounting in the world, and to let that seeing begin to transform the very way we approach and carry out the necessary and so often hidden tasks of family life.

I find myself evolving two principles I consider essential to parenting that is peace conscious. They may be stated as follows:

Let us not avoid contact with suffering or close our eyes in the face of suffering, especially that which results from war preparations and the possibility of war. Let us in every way possible awake ourselves to this terrible possibility.

Let us continually be aware of the radiance of each moment and the possibility in each moment to foster peace and compassion by the very way we respond to even the smallest tasks like changing a nappy, assisting a child with a homework assignment, preparing a meal.

One dimension of parenting among those who see parenting as a vocation in itself and as the centre from which one's contribution to peace and justice begins to find expression is the dimension of limits. We are daily faced with the reality that we cannot be in several places at once, especially when we must answer to so many of our children's needs. Yet embracing and respecting these limits is the first step to opening our lives to be used in a much larger way in connection with others around the world.

When we bathe our infant with total attention that says, 'You are infinitely precious and unique,' we are also saying, 'Because you are precious, so are all children. Because I desire to nurture and protect your life, I desire that all children's lives be thus nurtured and protected.' In the daily unfolding of that realization, both parent and child begin growing into peacemakers. One finds that the more one gives love to one's own children, the more one's heart and arms ache to extend love and life to other beyond one's own family.

To be a parent and to let oneself truly love is in many ways to let one's heart be broken. We have all experienced the vulnerability that love brings, and what one of us has not felt that quiet despair when one's child is ill or injured - that knowledge always lurking just beneath the surface that life and togetherness could unexpectedly be turned to death and separation. Facing the danger of nuclear weapons increases that despair and breaks one's heart all the more. But after all, doesn't a broken heart have more space to fill, more space to take others in, more illusions discarded, and allow us to find a myriad of ways to enlarge and sustain each other in the work for peace?

There are many ways to be involved as families in peace work. For me, one of the greatest gifts of parenting is that at every moment of the day or night there are occasions to act on the possibilities of love from which all peace-making must flow. Parenting is, after all, not a philosophical exercise but a constantly incarnated response to life. Noses to wipe, fingernails to cut - even the most ordinary tasks can become kernels of peace to be offered one's child. And who can say that it is not those very tasks done in mindfulness and caring that will give our children eyes and hearts that will help build the way of peace.

MOBI HO
first published in *Mothering Magazine*, vol. 33.

You are not God, why do you act like God to children?
You are not all knowing, why do you laugh
at children's ignorance?
You are not almighty, why are you annoyed at
children's helplessness?
You are not complete, why are you irritated at
children's shortcomings?
Look at yourself first and then look at the child.

from 'The Child' by Gijubhai

Wardens' Children

Early in 1986 Rachel and I came as wardens to the Quaker Meeting House in Colchester, bringing with us Jennifer, who had just passed her third birthday, and Edward and Peggy, fifteen month old twins. The move was the result of a nappy-dominated year during which we had re-thought our lives.

I had drifted into university administration and, because I had enjoyed what I was doing, had stayed in one job too long. Now for the first time in my life I was working mainly for the money, which did not make the hours any shorter; I was frustrated that I seemed to be missing out on some of the most rapid and exciting stages of the children's lives; that they were developing so fast that sometimes I felt like a stranger to them.

Meanwhile, Rachel had spent the year virtually imprisoned in the house. Whenever I had a holiday and was able to throw my efforts into the daily round there was more to do than we could cope with; the position Rachel had found herself in at home on her own was past my powers of imagining. And yet she was at a crucial point in her career having recently gained a Law degree and just been appointed to the UN Committee of Quaker Peace & Service.

This did not mean that a straight swap or rôle reversal was on the cards; even if it could have worked it would have simply inverted our positions and frustrations. We wanted to share in the upbringing of the children; we both needed more time for interaction with them, not simply feeding them and cleaning up after them; we both wanted to keep our minds active and do something useful in the adult world. The wardenship gave us this opportunity.

The Meeting happily agreed to fence off the secluded rear garden to provide a safe playing area, but even so questions were asked about the accommodation; could we possibly bring children up in a flat? Then and now we were far more concerned with whether Friends and others could bear the noise and mess of resident children than whether we could put up with accommodation far better appointed than that of a great many young families all over the country.

The fact that we have never regretted the decision to come here does not mean that we think we have found any answers, that we give any more time unselfishly to our children than many parents who have handled the question far less flamboyantly, that the time will not come for us to rejoin the mainstream. So little has really changed. Life is still too short; times still occur when one or both of us feel that we are neglecting and losing touch with one or other of the children.

Some problems were new; with us both at home most of the time there was scope for conflicts of approach which would not have been apparent had one parent been doing the daily child-minding. Often it was simply a case of length of fuse, each of us could be critical of the other's heavy approach only until cracking in turn. We discovered that we had to decide who was in charge at any particular time and try, at least in theory, not to undermine each other's authority.

The main effect on me has been to make me far more humble about child-rearing, less prone to be inwardly critical of the over-wrought or unresponsive mother on the Clapham omnibus, more impressed by the achievements of single parents or those who both work full-time. We used to toy with the idea of educating the children at home, so unhappy had been our own very different school experiences. When the time came, we were overjoyed to be able to ship them off to school and enjoy six hours peace each day; the children are blissfully happy at school and we are most impressed by what the staff there achieve.

What about the children themselves? We made our decision and must live with it, but is it fair to impose life in a

Quaker Meeting House on children who had no choice in the matter?

There have definitely been positive factors. Being thrown into an enormous extended family did wonders for the children's social confidence, and enabled them to take starting school in their stride. We consoled ourselves with the thought of the encouragement we were giving to other young families; whatever embarrassments their children might provide the wardens could be guaranteed to play them on-side. On the other hand it was a knife-edge; we did not want to think that the situation might arise where families might stay away lest our children set them a bad example or lead them astray.

From our own point of view, living on the spot we could not be frightened away, as I think parents of young families sometimes are. We persevered and now have three children who each individually - if not all together - have shown themselves capable of sitting soberly through an hour's Meeting for Worship. People see our children in Meeting now and we have to explain that it wasn't always so; that the price is months or years of noisy, fidgety children in Meeting.

As time has gone on, we have realised that we were guilty of projecting on to our children too much of our own aspirations for the Meeting. It is not reasonable to expect that they would particularly wish to make friends with the children of parents who expressed an interest in Quakerism, particularly once they were at school and had so many companions to choose from.

If anything our three have grown to resent the infringement of the other children of the Meeting on their territory on a Sunday morning. We had to recognise that it was not sensible to force the children to attend the Children's Meeting just because they live here. Other children have the option of staying away; we are more happily placed than most parents in that being under the same roof they can stay away while we both attend Meeting. What we have made clear is that there can be no half-way house. Either the children are at Meeting and co-operate in what is going on, or they stay at home.

We are confident that the time will come when of their own free will they will wish to be involved again in the activities of the Meeting, but are convinced that there should be no obligation upon them as warden's children to be so involved. We cannot allow our decisions to interfere with their free will. As they grow older they may not even wish to remain Quakers. I hope that we will be able to accommodate this, too, without stress should the occasion arise.

If it is part of our witness as wardens to display to the world Quakerly methods of child-rearing, then we fail abysmally. This afternoon my six year old 'Quaker' children launched a series of attacks on me in the Meeting Room, wielding plastic swords and yelling "surrender or die!"

I could not help recalling the time when I myself was six and was asked to draw a picture of a Bible story which had just been read to us at school. Finding me staring blankly at the paper, the teacher discovered that not only did I not have the faintest clue of how to draw it, I didn't even have any concept of a sword and so had been completely baffled by the story. Toy weapons never entered our house. My parents never raised a voice or a hand to me, save I am told once, when I promptly retaliated by going down with measles. So great was the shock that all memory of the incident has been completely obliterated from my mind. And yet they were, and are, anything but Quakers. Where do I, as a Quaker, fail?

The answer is probably nothing to do with Quakerism. I was an only child. Life was orderly, well regulated. My mother ceased work some time before I was born, and for the remainder of her life devoted herself exclusively to the home. Neither I nor my parents had to cope with the constant strife and argument of a household with three children - I cannot cope with it now!

I have heard parents agonising over whether they can be Quakers if they resort to hitting their children - 'What about the Peace Testimony?' This question causes me no problem. The non-violent approach is almost certainly right, even if it trivialises the peace testimony's reference to 'wars and strife and fightings with outward weapons', its context of the taking of human life, to apply it to the slapping of a child. I do not think that physical punishment gives anything but the wrong signals, or that it does anything for the character of the victim. And yet with three children there are times when I resort to the back of my hand without compunction, not for the sake of the child struck, not without a sense of failure, but as the quickest means of protecting one of the others from harm or annoyance.

The same overriding personal loyalty governs my attitude toward reconciling the demands of the wardenship with those of the family; if it makes me a poorer warden and a better parent I know that the priorities are wrong: 'He that loveth father or mother more than me is not worthy of me.' (*Matthew* 10,37), but I know also that I cannot yet accept that further step.

Child-rearing can never be something to be smug about. One never knows what life-long harm has already been done, what problems lie around the next corner. Sometimes I am praised as a parent, but I always hear such praise in the acute knowledge of how little of the truth the speaker knows; how uncharacteristic is what they have seen. I would trade all the praise - more importantly all the good opinions which lie behind the praise - if I could think that those who have seen me only in moments of frustration, unreasonableness, violence, could also recognise that what they see is not the whole story. The truth, as always, lies somewhere in between. We may be 'public Quakers', but that does not make us worthy of exhibition. Indeed I would consider it the gravest breach of faith to burden our children with the pressures of being anything but a private family.

DEREK BRETT

Extracts from
Living Together, Learning Together

I have spent quite a bit of time in the past several months thinking about the real reasons why I do home schooling with my children. Why are my kids downstairs doing gymnastics and laundry rather than in a classroom with other Friends and friends of Friends?

First I want to give a reason that is not reason-able. I feel that we were clearly led to home school. No matter how well or how poorly we have accomplished our goals, the process of doing home schooling has increased our contact with God's will for our lives. I cannot trace any really logical sequence that led us here - it was an idea that took hold of me before I had children.

I want to say a few negative things about myself and home schooling, mostly in answer to a great many comments I have received about it.

I am not patient. ('You must be so patient to teach your kids at home!') I may be growing toward patience, but it is not a notable characteristic of my personality. Ask my mother. Ask my kids. I look back over the past twelve years and see a lot of impatience on my part, to say nothing of yelling and screaming and pushing. It is not easy being with kids, and I have not made it easy on myself.

I am not burdened with this vast responsibility of teaching my kids. Maybe I should be? ('It is a big responsibility to be your kids' teacher as well as parent.') The premise with which I started out parenthood was simply that I was responsible for the education of my children until they were able to remove that responsibility from me. Contracting with other people or institutions to provide parts of their education has never meant to me that I was handing over the responsibility, but rather that I was making an agreement that my kids could get certain resources that way. In other words, the responsibility never leaves home until the child does.

Another attitude I have always had which keeps me from feeling burdened is the idea that children learn how to learn by watching other people learn. So my husband, Ed, and I have used home schooling as a wonderful excuse to explore new subjects and skills. Often the children get interested in the subject too, but whether they do or not, I am enjoying myself and learning something and they are watching me learn and enjoy. Furthermore, when the children ask questions I cannot answer, we can all take the opportunity to hunt together for the answer. Much of what we do is done side by side rather than as teacher-student.

I see myself more in the rôle of a reference librarian than a traditional classroom teacher. I answer questions and connect them with resources, not control the pace of their learning. I do make suggestions at times when I think they are heading for a big imbalance. This has meant that I have encouraged Ada to do more exercise and Hannah to do more academics than they would have chosen for themselves. But ultimately it is up to them.

I do not spend much time living in my children's future. This is perhaps the most radical idea of all. We all know parents who have chosen a future for their child and pushed him or her so much in that direction that they cannot enjoy the wonder of the child's present existence. My sense is to find out what the child needs now and enjoy that present process.

Now I would like to share a few positives.

Rather than being burdened with the responsibility for my children's education, I have come to enjoy my responsibility with them. From spelling ('How do you spell "stop nuclear bombs?"' Jesse asked me yesterday.) to social structures ('I am the leader around here for everybody but Chris and Eric and Jerome and the big bullies,' Hannah reported last week.) to deep philosophical commentaries ('When we go to meeting we should leave a bench for God,' Jesse remarked one day. I asked what would happen if all the benches were full. 'Well, then we could just sit on God's lap.') - it is wonderful as a parent to have the ability to respond to whatever comes up.

Our children are always giving us clues to their gifts, and we need to ponder them until we see a way to support and nurture those gifts.

What does it mean to support gifts of your children? I think the first, last, and most important part of it is to listen to them. By 'listen' I mean not merely hearing their words and noises but paying attention to their whole beings - what they do with their time, what excites them, what bores them, what scares them, who they like to be with. This is the only way we can gather information to 'store in our hearts.'

What are we educating our children for anyway? Are we after more and more knowledge in more and more subject areas? Or are we looking for wisdom? Are we looking for people who can be open to the leadings of the Spirit?

Isn't it interesting to think how 'the simple and the quiet, the natural and the plain' describes so well what we as Quakers feel pulled to? Could it be that we should be educating our children to be 'Bears of very little brain' rather than wise Owls, clever Rabbits, or complaining Eeyores? What would that mean? Maybe the ability to enjoy throwing sticks in the river, the openness to having hums come knocking on the door, the instinctive use of those things around us to rescue other people.

It may sound as if I am suggesting we simply throw out the traditional academic subjects. I am not suggesting that, but I am suggesting that they be placed in a better balance with the spiritual, emotional, creative, and intuitive skills which have been so severely curtailed in most schools.

KATE KERMAN

first published in *Friends Journal*, 15.4.85

The child likes to do things.
Let him wash his own hanky,
Let her fill her own cup,
Let him arrange the flowers,
Let her clean the plate,
Let him pod the peas,
Let her serve the food,
Let the child act,
And act at her own pace,
And act at his own wish.

from 'The Child' by Gijubhai.

THE FOLLOWING is a selection from some of the thoughts that were spontaneously written by Judith and Martin Ward at various times during the months that followed the sudden death of their three year old son, Matthew.

The people who phone us or call round have often put themselves out so much to ask how we are, that it is hard to avoid the temptation to show our gratitude by reassuring them. I really don't know how we would have coped without so much love and support, both from friends at a distance and the many people in Maldon who, despite knowing us for only a short time, have been so good to us. We feel, as you say, a shattering gap in our lives, and it helps to know that others realise how big the loss is, so we feel that we've been told we have every right to grieve.

I had problems with colleagues of the stiff upper lip tendency, but fortunately, because of the nature of my work, I can choose to spend time on my own out of doors on the job, and I found crying on my own was more healthy than not crying in company.

Over eight weeks now: several weeks since the awful realisation that this grief is not something which you recover from, not something from which you can get better, because the cause of it will never be overcome. Matthew will never come back. His little ghost is very vivid sometimes, to both of us. He is usually wearing his big, blue corduroy coat that he was so proud of, or the clown-like pyjamas covered in little brightly coloured somethings.

We've lived through the first week of the nightmare. We've lived through our own child's funeral and watched the grass grow long and lush on his grave. We've grieved for three long months, survived the ordeal of the inquest, learnt to 'cope' and 'behave normally', to avoid upsetting people, to go on living with Hannah and for her. We've done all this and yet there's no reward at the end of it. Don't we deserve to have Matthew back now? But life and death are not like that. All the coping and adjusting only take us further from him.

I must make more time for remembering Matthew, and grieving for him, during the day. I shouldn't need to do it at three in the morning, but it's too easy to keep going during the day.

It's easy to assume that other people will be expecting us to be 'getting back to normal' and to live up to those assumed expectations, whether they were real or not. Martin, of course, is continually 'normal' at work, but at least work *is* as normal. I am still living around the big hole left by Matthew's death, every minute of the day, and sometimes I need to acknowledge the strain and hurt of that more than I do. There *is* joy and wonder in life still, closeness and sharing, fun and laughter, but all of that life is lived on and around the edges of the gaping hole.

Matthew's fourth birthday. I couldn't help crying when I first saw that written down on a card. A friend told me he would be thinking of us today. When we came home there were flowers on the doorstep. Someone brought a little present for Hannah and a card and others brought a little candle in a soapstone box. It's meant a lot to have the day's emptiness and sadness acknowledged by other people. We have good friends. Yet again we've had cause to give thanks for them.

Where am I? Grieving - missing Matthew in so many ways. Wanting to show him things, share things with him, hear him saying, "Look, mum." Wanting to plan outings and holidays with him, share his discoveries and developing abilities, encourage him, love him, hug him, take care of him, comfort him, make him better.... On a very basic level I still have a desperate need to take care of him, to look after him, to show that I *do* take care of him. I *did* try.

Yes, I do still have a lot to give thanks for. Hannah is strong, healthy, happy, confident, loving, adventurous, and ready for a life of enthusiastic exploration. As I nurse my shattered confidence as a mother back to strength, I'll have to trust Hannah to show me the world through her eyes, just so long as I keep loving her and listening to her.

How has Matthew's death affected us as parents? I suppose we have lost confidence in ourselves, although Matthew's short life was such an abundantly happy one, and as part of that loss of confidence we find it difficult to look forward to the future for our family. But then Matthew lived for the moment, full of joy in the here and now, and made us do so too, so we never thought about what he was going to do when he grew up.

We desperately needed to hear Matthew's name spoken, and to look through pictures of him with other people. There is an absurdity about people's attempts to avoid mentioning the death or the life of our child which we could almost laugh at at times. Several people, desperately trying to suppress all thought of our lad called me Matthew in Freudian slips and were then terribly embarrassed. 'Oh dear.' I felt like saying once or twice. 'You've reminded me of Matthew and I'd almost forgotton about him until you said his name!' To refuse to remember is to kill the child all over again. I'm paraphrasing someone else there. I'm not sure who.

Matthew had asked why there was no garden at the playgroup which he went to, so we found mental rest in the physical exertion of creating one, with money which had been given in his memory. Much of the money was given by friends and colleagues for whom that was the only expression of sympathy they could make.

What of the God who is parent to us through this? I have never believed that the world works according to God's plans, and I cannot do so now. It would have taken so little divine intervention to save Matthew, and it could have been done so discreetly. God is just left helping us to pick up the pieces again.

THE FOLLOWING is some thoughts of a mother whose son, Martin, had died of leukaemia.

Nine years ago, our second child died of leukaemia at the age of four, after an eighteen month illness. I shall not write of his illness and death here (though I now think that might have been my need in the first months and years after the event) but of the ways in which I still feel I am his parent in a very living way now. I will also describe some resources I've had to call on, not simply to survive the unbearable, but to grow and use the experience to develop my life.

I would like it to clear that I make no generalisations, for I am convinced that experiences of all sorts are unique and that I cannot speak for all my fellow parents who have lost children. I do not presume to make assumptions for my husband's feelings either, which is why I do not use 'we'. The reality is, of course, that we have both been equally involved in the process of finding a new place for our son in our lives.

As time has passed since Martin died, I have sometimes been aware of two conflicting forces; one is the desire to hang on to my sadness because in that state I seem able to feel closer to my son; the other is a feeling I should leave it behind and move on, taking creative energy from this critical experience to bring something special to my life.

For some time after Martin's death I avoided my feelings, but this was in my effort to survive, particularly because I had a new baby three months later and then twins two years after that. But I think this period made me lose touch with myself, and despite living in a busy community and having many friends, I was lonely inside. It was, however, during this time, on the second anniversary of Martin's death, that my Meeting for Worship warmly encouraged us (my husband is not a Friend or attender but feels a sympathy for our way of worship) to hold a memorial Meeting for Martin in our home, at a point when I felt the lack of his not having had a Quaker funeral.

I think this flexibility and openness which Friends can have is something very precious and I am grateful that my need was understood and heard. It was good to be in our home for this memorial Meeting for many reasons, one being that we had moved very soon after Martin's death and this Meeting brought him into our new home.

Since it is now relatively rare for children to die, there seems some confusion over how Friends can support a bereaved family and, as a parent, I found it difficult to know how to express my grief or what sort of support I wanted. In different words, I did not know what was expected or how to behave.

'But surely,' you will ask, 'you react in whatever way comes naturally and the community accepts?'.... My response is, 'But what if you are afraid of being overwhelmed?' I can now see that the fact that I chose to control my feelings gave Friends the impression that I was strong and brave and more in need of admiration than support - an isolated pedestal from which it is hard to leap down and get the help that is really needed.

I do not think that I could have begun to grow from my experience of losing a child if I had not first come to face the depth of my feelings and brokenness. I could not relinquish some of my sadness without fully indulging in it first. At least, this is how it seems to me. And this is something I have only explored recently, partly through psychotherapy, particularly in family therapy with my husband.

It is understood now, I think, that far from the death of a child bringing a couple closer together, it can lead to division and even divorce because of the parents' contrasting ways of coping with loss. The following example from our lives would describe how difficult communication can be but how important it is.

It was the anniversary of Martin's death, some years after the event, and my husband and I went for a walk in the North Kent Downs. It was a particularly beautiful summer's day; the cornfields full of poppies and some sections of the walk through woods. I felt a longing to tell my husband about the last morning of Martin's life which I'd never dared say aloud before (my husband had arrived minutes after Martin's death). But as I stumbled to speak, I could feel that he didn't want to hear it then. It seemed that he wanted the simplicity and joy of being close to nature and to Martin, who was with us in spirit on this special day. I wished I could feel the same but I couldn't. I felt resentful and silenced and sad and thought alone of that last morning as my husband walked on ahead.

The sessions of family therapy have given us (my husband and myself) the time and a safe place to talk about our experiences as parents and have brought us closer as a couple than we have ever been. They have also made it possible to express and come to terms with some difficult feelings; for example, negative feelings towards the baby that was born so soon after Martin died, when I would have liked Martin back. The ways in which we describe our family experiences in the therapy sessions become transformed; it is as if the image of our family is reflected back with its strengths underlined so that we can take something powerful away with us.

The family is not just the sum of its living parts. A family has its history and memories and, in our family, Martin is part of that and has had great influence on our continuing family life, very much including the three siblings he never knew. I think, for example, of the children's sensitive personalities and of the fact that death has been a subject in our family often, in different guises, and that this is demanding on them but brings extra maturity rather than gloom. I am glad that Martin's part in shaping our family cannot be taken away and I treasure the things that members of the family say about him or in relation to him which are as if extending his existence.

A recent example involves my six-year-old daughter who asked me (not for the first time) why Martin died and how, and then she wanted to know what he had said as he died. Hearing that he had not spoken, she led me into a discussion of what he would have liked to say to his family and it was clear that she felt herself part of the family to whom he said goodbye, even though Martin died before she was born.

I am certain that my own Meeting could not have given me all the support I needed, not because of inadequacy and not simply because I think I needed the experience of trained therapists, but because in my lost way I could not always receive the opportunities offered. I was, myself, difficult to reach. I do not think that what I am describing is unique to bereaved parents. We perhaps all have moments when we would like our needs to be guessed without even having to work out what they are for ourselves. Now I do feel I can share more with my Meeting - after all this time.

I am now training as an art psychotherapist, a career I probably would have been drawn to without the experience I have described, because I am an artist and attracted to the idea of art as healing. But I think that because of the process of healing that I have been through myself I could be a better art therapist for having known powerlessness vividly and the need to adapt and find my inner strength. This new venture helps me to make some sense of what has happened and let the sense reach beyond myself.

ANONYMOUS

A Type of Quaker Parenting

I'm fifty years old now, and a single parent. If I've brought up my children in a Quaker-like way it's with no thanks to me but to the example I received from my Quaker parents.

I have a younger sister and an older brother. My sister and I often quarrelled, but played together too, supporting each other in new situations. We were disciplined by a restriction of privileges (no outing to...) or banished to another room to cool down, or my mother would look injured and I'd feel so guilty that I'd 'toe the line'. I don't remember my sister or me ever receiving physical punishment. My brother did not either except for once. He was always up to mischief with his pals. I don't know what heinous crime he'd committed but on one occasion my father took a slipper to his backside, in an upstairs bedroom. My sister and I were so upset that we howled outside the door in sympathy and caused such a commotion that my father never repeated such a punishment.

As a child I also witnessed my parents 'open door' attitude towards people of all cultures; no racial prejudice was apparent. They gave hospitality to many through the British Council during the last World War. I remember feeling very offended because I was asked to 'kiss goodnight' a Scottish gentleman I hadn't seen before in my life!

We had a maid, but my parents put themselves out to support her in time of trouble (she had a husband who drank and beat her, and she was often short of money). They kept contact with her, in friendship, when she retired until she died. So although we were 'middle class' I was taught not to be snobbish but appreciative of our comforts compared with many others.

Our pocket-money was restricted so that we lacked nothing essential but weren't able to spend extravagantly. Most of our clothes were home-made. We weren't allowed to be food-fads, being continually reminded of the fact that half the world was starving for what we might be turning our noses up at!

Even disliked foods must be tasted to get used to!

We weren't to waste anything; we were taught to preserve not destroy the possessions we had. We lived comfortably, with luxury, but certainly not simply, though we definitely learned that people were more important than material things. My parents were generous of their time or money to anyone in distress.

I view all these things as part of a liberal upbringing; a reaction from the strict Victorian era and what most present-day Quakers will have experienced, no doubt. Guidelines were many but rules were few. However there were some unwritten rules. Anger was unacceptable and even heated debate was curtailed. There was an avoidance of 'tricky' topics, like sex. This meant that at times there was a cover up of feelings that an honest facing might have helped. I never felt that my parents were dishonest with me but found it too difficult to be open minded about controversial issues. I took many years to learn to 'speak my mind' without feeling guilty. I feel that many Quakers today still have this problem.

This brings me to my first prerequisite of Quaker parenting, that of honesty. My children have had a lot of strange circumstances to cope with in their upbringing; living in community, abroad, losing their father, having a fostered sibling, etc, yet I feel that honesty has seen us through. I've had to think through why I've done something, or want to do something so as to explain it to them, and apologise when I've been wrong in some action. This doesn't mean that one tells them all one knows. Sometimes I've had complaints from my children that they've asked a question and I've launched into a long philosophical answer, which they didn't want! At any age we can only take so much of another's 'truth'.

I've left much unsaid, waiting until they've asked, but tried to create the climate that encourages them to say what's on their minds, in their own time. The difficulty is when something is said as one is going out of the back door or in the middle of something that requires much concentration! I'm not always very good at stopping what I'm doing and really listening!

As part of honest dealings with children I feel it's wrong to make promises (or threats) that one can't realistically keep.

I reckon that patience is the next prerequisite, especially if one has an over-talkative youngster or an uncommunicative teenager! Good humour is also needed. Some Quakers are too severe in mien, to my mind. Why don't we enjoy our youngsters more? My teenager exasperates me but keeps me on my toes and greatly entertained also! Observing them and adapting to their growth has seemed to me to be an exciting challenge.

Anyone reading this may now say that what has been suggested, any parent could do without being a Quaker. True, but all this is a foundation, I feel, of attitudes that encourage the awakening of the Spirit. We're told in *Advices I* that '...through example and training we help them (children) to recognise and obey the voice of God in their hearts, that they may be joyful and willing in his service'. My children attended children's classes in the Meetings we've belonged to, but drifted away in their teens finding other activities of more importance to them and not even convinced that there is a God. So they haven't yet recognised his voice.

I too fell away from Quakers in my early adult life, only returning when I had my own children, appreciating the extended family of a Meeting that supported me in helping me define my view of Quaker parenting. My three young adults now see my commitment to Quakers and know I have faith in God and that this is important to me. They see me going to activities that teach me to grow in my spiritual life. They see my frailties also, but that I still want to learn.

I'm glad that I have reasonably responsible young adults but I'm not worried that they are not actively Quaker at present. I bear in mind the continuance of the *Advice* I mentioned, '...that there is a unique potentiality in each human being as a child of God, and that the Holy Spirit may lead your children along paths which you have not foreseen'. I believe that they are in His hands and have always been so, even whilst my responsibility. They aren't aware of this. I hope that one day they may be.

I've not been the ideal parent. I remember smacking my boys and I regret it. I've preached that it's wrong to take life, yet I've not been a vegetarian nor brought them up as such. I've taught peaceful co-existence, yet they've seen me angry. We've never had family prayers as they didn't want them, yet they respect my own need for quiet times. I don't think Christian or Quaker parenting is about being perfect. I feel that it should incorporate a willingness to learn, from one's children too.

I still feel that honesty, patience, good humour and hopefulness, incorporated in one's love for one's children, make the best ingredients for Quaker parenting, stemming from the continual development of one's own faith. We have to '... remember our testimony that Christianity is not a notion but a way'.

E.A. Brown

A Conversation

I'm not sure if there's any point in doing this, because I don't think there was anything particularly different in my upbringing from that of most of my Friends.

Well I suppose we made quite a conscious effort not to be different. I remember when you were first at Primary School there were several families of Closed Plymouth Brethren at the school. The children didn't come to assemblies, weren't allowed to mix socially with non-Brethren children, and didn't celebrate Christmas or birthdays. You were very insistent that if being a Quaker meant being 'different' as the Brethren, you didn't want to be a Quaker.

So we weren't really any different.

Not outwardly, no. Perhaps I was more conscious of differences at that stage, things like life-style, material values...But didn't your friends want to know what the difference was, when they knew that you were a Quaker?

Not really. Remember. it was a school with quite a lot of different nationalities and different religions. Very few people knew that we were Quakers, or would have been interested. I don't remember talking about religion to my friends, unless they were Quakers too. Even now, my other friends are almost totally disinterested in my Quaker activities or beliefs.

How do you think you felt about Quakerism? Do you remember resenting it?

That's really hard to answer, having known nothing else all my life. I just accepted it, like being British. I don't think I felt any resentment, or embarrassment, or any very strong reaction. It was just 'us'.

But I was conscious of differences, although they were probably quite similar to the experiences of any Christian parent trying to bring up children, I think Quakerism had a particular influence on the way we behaved towards you.

In what way?

I think it was the strongly pacifist ideals of Quakerism which we interpreted as covering every eventuality from potty training to nuclear warfare. It meant that we tried to be very liberal, very egalitarian, in the treatment of our children. For instance, we tried to use co-operation rather than confrontation to discuss issues, to respect your views. You know my favourite text, 'a soft answer turneth away wrath.'

Yes, I've heard you quote that hundreds of times! It sometimes really annoyed me, all that peaceful stuff!

Do you think you would have preferred us to have been very strict, very authoritarian parents?

No, not really. But I'm very strong-willed anyway, and perhaps it wouldn't have made much difference. I guess I would have turned out much the same either way.

But I can't help wondering if it would have been easier for me as a parent; conflict avoidance can be very wearing! I think the other major difficulty is one which faces any parent trying to balance family responsibilities with commitment to the wider community, and that's just trying to fit things in. So often I felt that we were in danger of getting the balance wrong, and I was constantly guilty about neglecting one side or the other. We seemed to be very involved with Meeting and meetings.

No, that isn't my childhood memory. I don't think you were out or away so much then as you are nowadays. Now I think you are much too involved in Quaker things, they seem to take up a lot of time.

Do you mind?

No, except when I see you getting very tired. But I understand why you are involved, and because I share your views on peace issues and social concerns, and because I'm totally in sympathy I can hardly complain.

It's really great that you feel the same way as we do, but I suspect that your views don't stem entirely from your Quaker upbringing, do they?

No, I don't think so - I think it's something I would have worked out for myself. You didn't put any pressure on me to conform to Quakerly ways, I just happen to feel at home with them.

Do you think that's why you are still 'with us', because you feel at home in Quakerism?

I suppose so. Quakers are the people I relate to most easily, especially as we live in a town where I don't find many like-minded people. But it's probably involvement with the

Leaveners, going to Junior Yearly Meeting, and finding others of my age with the same life-style, the same ideals, which has been the most important factor.

What do you like least?

I get cross with the image of Quakerism, but not from outside, from inside, the sort of stereotyping of ourselves which makes some people seem obsessed with 'being Quakerly' - keeping up the loving, caring, peaceful exterior. Sometimes that seems to be too good to be true to me! And I don't like talking about my spiritual feelings; I can't analyse my reaction to Meeting for Worship, for instance, it's too personal, too precious to explain. Quakers are forever trying to get to the meaning behind things, I'm just not into all that deep stuff!

Do you think you would want your children to be Quakers?

Only if they felt completely happy in it.

As you do?

As I do.

BETH CANTRELL

Instead of going to your club take the child to the park.
Instead of gossiping show the child some animals.
Instead of being immersed in your newspaper,
Listen to the child.
When the child goes to bed delight her with stories.
Take interest in the child.

from 'The Child' by Gijubhai

A Quaker Parent

My mother died last year, at the age of seventy-five, and after a long illness. As our family went through this process together, the values which she and our father had taught us were lived out in our automatic reactions and in our conscious responses.

There were, originally, four of us Bailey children, myself, Cherry, Ruth and Chas, then five when Martin Newing came as a long term foster child. We are fairly spread out in age with a fourteen year gap between me and Martin, but we were trained to do important things together, and so when Mum first became suddenly and seriously ill we all travelled to meet around her bedside and to support each other and Dad. Martin was overseas during this time, but kept in touch by phone and made a special visit to England to say goodbye. Unwritten, but clearly understood family principles prompted us. When we met the first time, the silent grace before our meal was deep and prolonged. We didn't hesitate to be cheerful and enjoy each other's company, even though the reason for us being together was sad - we could accept the mixture of happiness and anxiety.

Incidentally, food was important through these two years - a basic family principle was 'bring something to eat together and leave something for Dad'. Is this religious or just human? The root meaning of 'religious' is from *religare* which means to bind together. Eating Chas' cheesecake and Cherry's potato salad certainly linked us up, as did our silent grace beforehand.

We had always learnt to give to the Meeting and to call on the Meeting for help - and Friends, to whom she had given so much, gave her so much in return, especially in the last five months of her life. Meals, visits, cards, thoughts and prayers all flowed.

Edna Bailey wasn't a passive recipient of all this! After her first serious illness. She might have become a quiet old lady sitting by the fire - but I don't think she was actually capable of that - instead she decided, with the children of Bradford-on-Avon Meeting, to produce *Toad of Toad Hall* in the Meeting car park. Mum's productions illustrated her values. Each child that wanted one had a part. Each one was individually coached and shown how this part fitted into the production. Each one's potential as the Chief Weasel, or Lucy Rabbit, of Alfred, or Ratty, was sought and brought out. The vision of a corporate production was created from a lot of individual visions, held in the minds of all, and made real on a sunny afternoon in the car park. She had been producing plays with Meeting children for thirty years. She said once, 'Children are my life.' However, her parenting of other people's children did not feed off them emotionally; her aim was a child's independence and self-determination. She also gladly received much ministry from children, and rejoiced in it.

Three days after the play she had a small stroke, and a week later another, bigger one. Undoubtedly the terrific effort of *Toad of Toad Hall* contributed to these - but she believed in living life abundantly and giving abundantly, whatever the cost. This cost was acknowledged and accepted without bitterness by her family, the choice an individual makes being sacrosanct.

Looking back at the last five months of her life, I pick out truthfulness and quietness as the important values which we learnt from her and Dad as children, and which we all lived by during that time. It was taken for granted by now that we gathered at crucial times and that we all contributed food or skills as was needed. We did not pretend to ourselves or to our children that she was going to get better. We brought the young ones in the family to say goodbye, and each had ten minutes or so alone with her. Like the actors in *Toad*, each grandchild knew that they were special and much loved.

Our family relationships have always been based on truth - not shouted but recognised - and being truthful with Mum about what was happening to and in her helped her to be truthful about her fear and her sadness - and then to let them go into quietness. We talked of the afterlife. Dad's scientific objectivity and weighing of the evidence was useful. Mum refused to speculate, saying, 'I just don't know.'

Gradually the outside world fell away. The last item of world news she noticed was that Gorbachev (always a pin-up) was reducing expenditure on armaments. The eternal took over from the finite and temporal - flowers, songs, pictures and people were more important - money, politics and committees were forgotton. In our early years, she put effort into making happy times for us - Christmases, parties, holidays - and now we spent happy times recalling them. She approached death calmly, and like her, we now feel that death is no barrier to the living.

In the end only the presence of love mattered. Our shared experience of that love down the years now binds us more closely to her and to each other.

BETH ALLEN
(with help from the rest of the family)

Children, obey your parents, for it is right that you should. 'Honour your father and mother' is the first commandment with a promise attached, in the words: 'that it may be well with you and that you may live long in the land'.
You fathers, again, must not goad your children to resentment, but give them the instruction and the correction which belongs to a Christian upbringing.

Ephesians 6:1-4

Quaker Parenting

I have been a Friend for four years now, and when I asked my teenage children what difference they had noticed in my parenting, the answer came back quickly, 'none'. This set me wondering why. If, as I think, I have changed a lot since becoming a Friend, why had it not affected my parenting in any way?

One reason could be that I have always been a Christian, and had always tried to bring them up with a Christian background and with Christian morals and ethics. I had always treated them with respect, and, as they got older, with equality, as I felt it was important not to be an authoritarian figure, as my parents had been, but to be more of a friend who they could actually come and talk to whenever they had a problem or just wanted a chat.

As I looked at their friends and the problems that they had had with their parents, I felt that, just as communication between parents is important, communication between parents and children is possibly the most important part of parenting after the demonstration of love. It can be very hard to say 'I love you' as children get older, but it can be even harder to give them cuddles and kisses and make them feel loved. I think one of the greatest gifts you can give a child is sharing your time and listening to them whenever they want to talk. As with adults, just talking things out can sometimes help so much, yet so many children are not listened to and are pushed into the background of parents' lives.

Another reason, possibly, more relevant to Friends, is the fact that I had always been a pacifist and hence would not use corporal punishment on my children. Talking to my older children about this, I discovered that my method of discipline apparently had more terror for them than the fear of being smacked. I am not sure if I read about this form of punishment or thought it up myself, but it came just as my eldest son was at the stage of needing some discipline, and I was wondering how best to resolve conflicts without resorting to smacking.

It is simply a matter of, when the child is naughty, making them stand still by a door. I have used this method for over twenty years now, and my eldest son, who is now twenty-two, assures me that just the memory of it still fills him with dread. Especially useful in this system was the degree of punishment - you either stood by the back door, and inside door, or, worst of all, the front door. The added deterrent of this was the fear of being seen by an arriving visitor through the glass panes of the door, before I had the chance to answer it. This really had an impact on the older children, and I believe still does on the youngest who are twelve, and although I use it much less nowadays, as there is not such a great need, I believe the deterrent effect is still there.

The length of time they stood by the door was determined, more or less, by their age. For the younger child, one or two minutes was a long time, whilst as they got older five, ten or fifteen minutes (in very serious cases) would not be untoward. The main thing was that they were not allowed to lean or talk to their brothers or sisters or anyone else.

Possibly, this may have something to do with their now being able to go to Meeting for Worship and sit still for the whole hour, only reading intermittently. So although I have only recently come to Friends it may be that the grounding was there in my parenting for a long time.

ANGELA PERRETT GREEN

A Lesbian Perspective

All my adult life the desire to be a mother has been strong in me. This is so for many women and for most of them it is easily fulfilled. For me it was somewhat different, as I am a lesbian.

I began to live with my partner, Pat, when I was twenty-five and for the first ten years of our relationship I coped with my feelings by working as a Child Care Officer, by filling the house (and a field) with animals, and by living in a sort of fantasy world whereby I almost believed that a knight on a white charger would come galloping along, magically change me into a heterosexual woman, and give me loads of babies!

By the time I was thirty-five we had two dogs, three cats, several cows, pigs, goats, chickens, ducks and two donkeys. I was enjoying my job but, as I became more senior, moved further away from actually handling children, and the knight had not arrived.

At work I was desperately seeking a foster home for a small girl of two who was mentally and physically handicapped. It dawned on us gradually that I could be her foster mother and, after all the usual preliminaries, I gave up my job and she came to live with us. At the same time I fostered numerous short-term children, amongst them pre-adoption babies, and my joy was complete when one of those babies, who arrived at nine days old, never left us. I was able to adopt her just after her first birthday.

These two children form our permanent family but, in addition to them, we have cared for fifty-two foster children over the years. For eight years we had a group of particularly difficult children and Pat joined me in giving them full time care. This work came to a natural and a gradual end as our own two girls reached their teens.

It is strange looking back, but in those early years the fact that I was a lesbian did not feature very much. In those days we lived in a close-knit rural community in Cornwall where, by virtue of our distance from the rest of the world, we were interdependent on one another. Pat and I were accepted just for ourselves, and then as our growing family arrived they were accepted and integrated too. Maybe we were thus cocooned from the real world, or maybe homophobia was not so strong as it has become.

As for my own self I was too busy being a mother to worry very much about being a lesbian for I found that the desire to mother had not been a fantasy. It was something I enjoyed and was good at and I found myself fulfilled. Furthermore, by the very virtue of the fact that we were not a stereotyped family, Pat and I were able to help some very disturbed children who had been horribly damaged by their own more conventional families.

In recent months there has been some controversy about lesbians becoming foster and adoptive parents. It has felt very strange because, of course, to us, as to our girls, it all seems so natural. We do not see ourselves as somehow set apart and the thought that we should have been denied children because of our sexuality I find extremely hurtful. Our family life is little different from anyone else's. We have moved to the Midlands, but are just as well integrated into the local community (Pat is even Clerk to the Parish Council). We are active in our Meeting and we do the same sort of things as other people.

I think it is the failure to see us as individuals which causes problems to those who would deny us the right to have children. Being good at mothering is an individual skill - some women are good at it, others are not. Those abilities are not linked to sexuality at all. It is the amount of love and security which one can give a child and one's ability to help him/her to grow up confident in her/his own self worth that is important.

Being a lesbian mother does, however, require special skills. One has to be aware of the lack of a male rôle model and find ways of compensating for this. In our own case we were lucky to have Pat's parents living nearby so that our children had a close relationship with a 'Grandad' right from the start. In addition to that we made sure that they experienced family life in heterosexual households where they were invited to stay.

Sadly, one has to accept and prepare one's children for the fact that they may meet prejudice. We chose to do this by being completely open about our relationship in every area of our lives so that they do not feel it is something which has to be kept secret or hidden. In this way we hope to protect them from ridicule at school and our experience in this area has been positive. It is secrecy and fear which do the damage.

Some people express the anxiety that being brought up by lesbians will somehow affect the children's psycho-sexual development or give them a problem with gender identity. All the research that has been done (mostly in America although a significant study has been carried out at the London Institute of Psychiatry) has shown this is not so. Children brought up by lesbians tend to grow up much like other children and to be equally stable.

Some people believe that being brought up by lesbians may influence the children into being lesbian or gay themselves. Statistics do not bear this out! All our own lesbian and gay friends and acquaintances are the products of heterosexual households and again research shows that there is no significant difference between the children of lesbians and those of heterosexual women.

It is reassuring to have the research findings so that what we know instinctively is validated in fact. It would be a tragedy indeed if lesbians were banned from fostering and adoption. It would be sad for those lesbians who, like myself, feel a strong need to be mothers. It would be even more sad for those children who wait for families and whose needs could be met in a lesbian household. There is a great diversity of need in children awaiting homes and that can best be met by keeping the vetting procedure as open and as wide as possible and by assessing each applicant on their ability to parent which is, after all, what it is all about.

As for myself, I have never regretted my decision to become a mother, and so far, at least, our girls do not feel that they have been disadvantaged by being placed with us. I try desperately not to force them into sex-stereotyped roles, but I am longing desperately for the next stage - the grandchildren.

JUDITH WEEKS

The Primrose Line

'... Do hope that you will enjoy your visit to the Primrose Line and take home with you some fond memories.'

This announcement was made on the steam train trip during our summer holiday, a holiday that was already going far from well. The 'fond memories' of this day are not all that fond. Our teenage son was behaving badly and my feelings of resentment and anger, attached to a weariness about bothering at all were fairly great. Our son and his friend were being silly, almost to the point of abuse, had refused to put on cagoules even though it was a day of torrential rain and were rushing about on the train, refusing to sit anywhere near us and showing off.

Meanwhile, around me in the train I could hear voices, parental ones. 'It's your teeshirt. It's your responsibility...Look at you! However did you get it on you? It looks like oil.' and 'Sit down, be quiet, both of you and look out of the window.'

The Primrose Line brochure said...'as the train stops for a few minutes on its return journey...' so I stepped out to look at the Victorian branch-line station. The boy opposite us across the gangway, aged about nine, also stepped out, missed his footing and fell heavily, his head towards the platform and feet still in the train. He was lucky not to fall between the two. His parents immediate reaction was of anger, mixed with reassurance and concern.

'Sit down. Where did you hurt yourself? If you had sat still this would never have happened. You should have stayed in your seat...I told you...when you're in a train you stay in your seat until it's time to get off.'

All around me were parents seeking control of their children. I did not feel so isolated, but it set me thinking about my rôle as a parent.

'Write about the joys, traumas, challenges, insights or revelations of being a Quaker parent,' said the letter in *The Friend*. Well, I've seen all those in the last sixteen years. Joy was there on becoming an adoptive parent, trauma on discovering our daughter's severe medical condition. The challenge came when adopting again and the revelations when knowing that sometimes we just could not cope.

Learning how to be an effective parent goes on and on, a learning which for me has been very revealing and given me insights into those parts of me which I did not care to discover. My experience has not been an easy one, but yet I feel very privileged to have been allowed to bring up someone else's children.

First came the time when I wondered if I could ever become a mother and realised over the months and years that perhaps I never would become a natural parent. Those traumatic years spent attending an infertility clinic brought moments of raised hopes and others of despair. We were lucky to be accepted as adopters fairly quickly, though a longer time had been spent finding an agency whose lists were not closed.

Our daughter, who came to live with us at twelve weeks old, was an easy baby, delightful toddler and young child and is normal enough as a teenager. No hassle, you would think, except that caring for a child with a serious blood disorder is a very taxing rôle. Days and nights have been interrupted by sudden bleeds and the need to rush off to hospital for treatment. Days have been spent sitting by a hospital bed, wondering whether the treatment will work, wishing her well again and thinking how to fit in the other demands of a family life, housework, shopping, cooking and so on.

Add to this the experience of being allowed to adopt again, this time a lovable little four year old, an energetic, almost hyperactive little boy, exploding into our lives and bringing with him all the emotional hang-ups of a disturbed early childhood. Our son has brought us an amazing amount of hardship and worry as well as a good deal of fun and pleasure and I've learnt a lot about how not to be a parent, while struggling to keep control of many situations.

How should I have reacted when feeling angry, frustrated and physically exhausted? Those elements of gentleness, compassion and understanding which I want to apply have flown out of the window. No wonder I had times of great guilt feelings. Entrusted with the care of children not born to you gives a heightened sense of responsibility and the feeling that you must 'get it right', while always being more conscious of the approval of others. Adoption need not bring difficulties and can be and is a wonderful experience.

I feel very close to my children, perhaps closer than some parents feel towards their natural children. I have tried to give them a sense of warmth and belonging, a feeling that they are loved and respected. They both know about their adoptions and if and when the time comes when they wish to know more than we can tell them about their backgrounds. I hope we shall be able to help and support them. Our extended family has always been totally supportive of our children, which has helped them to 'belong' through their growing years. Over the years too, we have come to see that the Meeting supported us like an extended family, propping us up in times of need and being available with advice and care.

So what is it like being a Quaker parent? It's very hard work if you take your rôle seriously and act responsibly towards your children. I hope our two have learned that tolerance of others in this world is important and that caring and compassion are good feelings. The fight against the wanting of too many material goods has been difficult, as those deprived of early love crave more possessions. I hope too, that a respect for all God's creation has been instilled along with the knowledge that war is evil and wrong and only causes suffering.

My experience does not make me bitter. I continue to look for the good things in life and feel a sense of pride and encouragement when my children excel themselves, whether it be through some small act of thoughtfulness, performing well in a school play or while speed skating at the roller rink. The good times always seem to balance the bad times.

And so to the Primrose Line again. Though it was not all sunshine and flowers on the trip, after a while our son and his friend began to take an interest in the journey and later managed to don their cagoules. Presumably the oily tee shirt owner was forgiven and, maybe, mother applied a stain killer to the offending mark. I hope the boy's fall did not lead to concussion or further headache. I realised that I had a lot to be thankful for. Being a parent is an experience I would not have missed.

JULIET BATTEN

Let parents and teachers realise that by threats and bribes
you cannot teach children good conduct,
they will only be ruined.
By threats you make a child rough;
By bribes you make a child covetous;
Threats and bribes make a child shameless and pitiable.

from 'The Child' by Gijubhai

Types of Parenting

What is a parent? I have always been confused. Not being a product of a nuclear family: mummy, daddy and 2.4 children, I read and listen to stories of family life with an envious, frustrated ear.

I am not a parent but I am a product of multi-faceted parenting. I can boast about five parents and numerous other individuals and institutions that shaped me thoughout my childhood and adolescence. As an adult approaching 30 I am only just beginning to recognise the riches of my experience, the pain and the joys. I long to talk to and read of others who have not been products of a nuclear family. We need to develop ways of supporting each other towards an under-standing and acceptance of a chaotic family history.

There must be lots of people like me. Increasingly, the myth of the nuclear family as a norm and as an ideal is being exposed. As a society we need to create and celebrate new ways of living together, new ways of parenting.

I was born in 1960 to parents whose marriage rapidly disintegrated under many pressures including severe personal crises. The precise details and dates of the story elude me, but I have put together over the years a kind of revolving jigsaw, to which I continue to add.

At about the age of five I spent six months with my grandmother in Wales, far away from my home ground in eastern England. When I returned it was to live with foster parents in the village where I was born. These people became my family until the age of eleven when I went to a Quaker school as a boarder.

My time with my foster parents provided me with a crucial stability and predictability into which each of my parents descended periodically to take me out or take me on holiday. I was very confused as to who were my real parents, at one point being convinced that my foster family were and these visitors were imposters. I cannot look back on that time as happy. I increasingly recognise and remember that I was a very unhappy child full of powerful feelings of needs which I felt I could not express for fear of losing what security I did have. These feelings are only now beginning to surface in consciously identifiable ways.

So, on to a boarding school which very much became my parent as did certain individuals within it. I was made a ward of court with the school acting *in loco parentis*. The school became another 'parent' whose approval and acceptance I desperately needed. I thus pursued a career of doing everything in school -music, drama, sport, academic studies, being Head Girl with a terrifying sense of urgency. Fortunately, I gained a lot of success through these activities and they formed a creative way of dealing with much of my unconscious distress and dislocation.

I wonder if some of the teachers there realised the full power of their 'parenting' and shaping of me as an individual. There the Quaker philosophies planted themselves firmly into my personality as guiding lights. I was led into Quaker activities such as workcamps (now QISP) and the Leaveners. These became a vital part of my parenting as I began to feel part of an extended family, with a coherence, loving acceptance and creativity that met many of my still undefined but strongly felt needs.

Through my adolescence I saw my parents sporadically. I had strong negative feelings about my mother which I could not understand at the time but now I recognise as a response to her emotional distance as well as physical distance from me. She underwent enormous financial sacrifices to put me through the Friends School which was able to parent me in a way she couldn't. When I was nineteen she went mad and I discovered a history of secret alcoholism which had helped to precipitate this.

Throughout my university career I was back and forth to Cambridge, while my mother was in and out of mental hospitals. Being an only child I lacked the support other siblings could have provided. My foster parents and my village remained a vital point of reference during this time. I still visit them and their love and support continues to be a source of security.

My mother is now well and we are beginning to build a relationship built on respect and understanding; both of us are now far more available to the other than ever before.

My father, meanwhile, left the country in 1971 when I was eleven, marrying and starting a new family. He lived abroad until 1989 when he returned to live in England. During that time I went to visit him once or more a year, but our relationship remains for me an uncomfortable mixture of a deep emotional and physical closeness and a superficial knowledge and understanding of each other's lives. We have yet to establish any real dialogue about our relationship and particularly his early parenting of me and his subsequent departure.

I suspect that I have a deep well-spring of anger and bitterness towards my natural parents which I have still not recognised, let alone expressed. I am beginning to see that

I am acting out patterns of behaviour and relating in my adult life which owe a lot to my experience of parenting. Until I render conscious many of the feelings and thoughts from this experience I fear I will continue to act them out in a variously chaotic and sometimes creative way.

I recognise that my experiences are not unique, although the specific combination may be. What I want to do is to allow myself all the feelings and thoughts I may have repressed, both negative and positive, so that I can celebrate and mourn my lack and my experience of parenting. Maybe I will be a parent, but this journey of understanding is vital to me, whether I become a parent or not.

ANONYMOUS

Adoption

At first it all seemed so straightforward. We married. We tried unsuccessfully for four years to have our own children. Adoption was, at that time, a practicable alternative, and we waited only ten months before being offered a baby boy. Adam was six weeks old when we first took him home with us; three months later he was legally 'ours'. He gave us much joy and fulfilment.

Two years later we adopted Helen. The family was complete, both children were beautiful, healthy, well-behaved and apparently perfectly adjusted.

From the beginning, our Adoption Society had told us that Adam's mother was passionately concerned for his well-being and continued to ask for reports of his progress. This we felt happy to do - and from time to time we sent photos and letters to show her how well he was doing. These were channelled through the Adoption Society - we had no direct contact with her. I never told Adam of this indirect link with his birth mother.

Helen's mother, on the other hand, had behaved in the more usual way, severing all contact with the Adoption

Society as soon as we took Helen home. Helen was about seven when she asked me how she ought to feel about her birth mother. 'Shall I love her because she was my real mother or shall I hate her because she didn't want me?' Although I tried to assure her that both feelings were natural and that she was bound to feel an ambivalence, she finally chose to hate her natural mother and only referred to her in derogatory and dismissive terms. 'You are my parents' - she would say - 'There isn't anyone else.'

Early childhood was happy. Adam was always an affable and easy-going child. He seemed to weather all storms, he did well at sports, music and art and although not an academic high flyer, he did well enough. Emotionally, he was as undemonstrative as most boys - but we enjoyed and shared his lively sense of humour. Helen was never as easy. Retrospectively she assures me that she remembers her childhood as 'idyllic' but she was a strongwilled and often difficult child, always a leader, full of character - the sort of child admired and enjoyed by teachers but exhausting to her family.

When Adam became eighteen we felt constrained to tell him what we knew of his birth mother. By this time we had learned that she had subsequently married Adam's father, that she had another son (Adam's full brother) but that her marriage had eventually failed. I also knew that she longed to meet Adam, and felt that he should know this. He took the information calmly and his first thought was to ask how we would feel about this. We assured him that it would be alright by us and after some months Adam initiated contact (through the Adoption Society.) He eventually met his mother and then his sixteen year old brother. It must have been quite an ordeal for him but he carried it off with his customary *sangfroid* and although I have to admit to some mixed feeling and strong emotions on my part - I felt the rightness of the meeting. Adam assured us more than once of his commitment to us and his gratitude for being part of our family. I have now met his mother and brother. That was also a highly charged but deeply satisfying meeting and I have formed a close friendship.

For Helen, however, this was too much to bear. She was extremely hostile to the whole venture, she accused Adam of jeopardising our family solidarity, of betraying us as his parents and of rejecting her as his sister. Nothing would reassure her, she set her face against it and refused to discuss her feelings. This reaction is perhaps hardly surprising, both in view of Helen's childhood decision to reject her own mother but also because, when she was eighteen, Helen herself became pregnant.

Although in many ways, we felt a certain sense of inevitability about it, this was as much a sense of shock and grief as it must be to any parent in that situation. Helen's adolescence had been stormy and exhausting, she always seemed drawn to friends whose influence was to say the least, unfortunate. She got into various scrapes, she lied, she played truant, she stayed out late and was generally an extremely uncomfortable person to live with. In many ways, the pregnancy represented the ultimate act of defiance.

They were hard months. Helen made an early and firm decision that she would have the baby adopted ('after all, I was adopted, and I was a success' she said!) She also insisted on total secrecy - which was difficult, complicated and extremely wearing. It also removed any possibility of sharing the burden, either for Helen or us. It was a particular sorrow for me not to be able to share the pain with my parents and other close friends. Helen cut herself off from all outside contact and for the last two months we lived in a state of self-imposed siege.

It was, however, a greet time of growing together for Helen and me. We talked as we hadn't done for some years, we shared our pains and our deepest feelings about each other. But this had a bitter corollary, in that because of my closeness with Helen, both my husband, Tom, and Adam felt hurt and excluded. This sense of exclusion has been hard to reverse - only now - two years on, am I gradually feeling closer to Adam again and aspects of my relationship with Tom also needed re-building.

The baby was born, (I was there) and Helen managed the whole thing with admirable strength and determination. She never wavered in her decision to have her daughter adopted and she made a huge effort to look forward and plan a new future for herself. The counselling which we all received was of a high quality and very supportive, it even led us to feel that the whole experience - despite its sadness and pain - had been a growing and learning point for all of us.

That was two years ago. After giving up the A level course upon which she had embarked when she became pregnant, Helen now has a job as a nanny to two small children, where she feels 'happy and fulfilled' (her words.) Although I was concerned that her reasons for taking this job might have been in some way an expression of her own denied mother-hood, she copes in a very objective manner and is naturally good and patient with small children (which never ceases to amaze me!) She is, however, quite adamant that she would not expect or want her daughter to come looking for her when she reaches eighteen.

As parents, Tom and I feel we have been through a pretty rigorous training! We have seen adoption from more than one angle, and although of course birth parents can have just as many tribulations (and more) we feel we have been presented with some tough challenges. There have been times of pain, fury, exasperation and even despair. I suspect that it has been particularly hard for Tom. Helen has always demanded (and too often got) my total attention. It has taken time for all four of us to learn to trust each other again. Unconditional love has, I am convinced, to begin with oneself; it is a very hard concept to pass on.

And, of course, we are not only parents but grandparents. There was never any question of Helen keeping her baby but I had more than a few pangs of sadness at the realisation that we were losing (for the moment anyway) the chance of this particular relationship. The fact that the baby was not a 'real' grandchild was at times a comfort, but mostly it made as little difference as the fact that I am not Helen's 'real' mother.

Discussions between parents - particularly at the teenage level often throw up such remarks as 'nobody told me it would be as bad as this' or 'if I had known it was this difficult I would never have had children.' I think I have discovered that although the expectations of parenting (like marriage) may be commonly held, the actual experiences are unique to every single family. All the textbooks and instruction manuals in the world will not solve the particular and individual situations with which parents find themselves confronted.

It is hard to know whether our Quaker approach has been of a very different kind to that of other Christian parents. Probably we were less inclined to strict unquestioned discipline, perhaps we relied too much on an intuitive response to problems. There were undoubtedly times when finding 'that of God' in a truculent and obstinate teenager gave us much food for thought.

ANONYMOUS

Extracts From
Coming to Terms with Folk-Tale Truths

Folk tales, like dreams, are often about feelings deep inside and perhaps otherwise hidden: they are not about actions out in the open. I have had to learn to come to terms with the existence of some of those feelings during several years of being a step-parent in an affectionate, caring family. They are *nasty* feelings, which the folk tales begin to touch on, to clothe and give expression to. When I first found these feelings in myself, I was glad to remember the tales, sharing as they do the experiences of countless step-parents and step-children through generation after generation. I have been fortunate to be able to talk with an elderly, wise social worker. She was able to tell me, from her own wide experiences, that many people nowadays have just the same problems, in various degrees of intensity. That was even more comforting.

What nasty feelings? For example, I have learnt what it is to feel bitter envy of the special relationship between my step-children and their 'real' parent. I know what it is to feel hurt beyond reason at being excluded from this relationship, not carelessly or wilfully, but simply as a fact of life. I have experienced within me overwhelming, sickening hate. These feelings, especially the last, are terrifying. They are not a part of my everyday emotions. But they appear from time to time, unheralded and unsought, from some place within me which I had not known before. I do not think they affect my actions a great deal. I do not banish the children to starve to death - though they do not get so close to me as the child who has since been born to me. I do not give that little child treats denied to his big step-brothers and sisters - at least, not big ones....

These 'nastinesses' used to make me feel miserable and desperately guilty. But slowly, over the years, that has changed. It is partly that I now know that I am not alone in having such feelings inside me. But it is mainly that I have

come to accept that I cannot by will alter those feelings. I can usually use my will, however, to control my actions. Of course I fail at times. I say the hurtful words, I snub the child, brush him or her aside. But the bad moment passes, and there is a moment of grace, when it becomes possible to start again - the child comes to ask a question, or I am making cakes and can ask the child to stick the cherries on the top, or we share a television programme.

I wonder whether the meaning of the Cross is not contained in all this, stripped of all allegory. What is done is past and nothing can alter it, so that in a special sense we no longer bear responsibility for it, and because of that we need carry no guilt. We *do* bear responsibility for our actions *now* and in the future, to be open to grace, and to use our wills more sensitively in situations which are at least in part the product of our past actions. It is a tremendous relief to me to be able to make a decision about things that matter now, without feeling that I must in addition be making reparation in some way for my past actions. I am not escaping from the past: one of the things that matters now may be the raw feelings of a child I have recently snubbed. But in shedding the guilt, I can concentrate on the child and forget myself.

All of this is written from my point of view as a step-parent. I have not yet found the right time - or the courage - to talk about such things with my step-children. Certainly the children do have nasty feelings to come to terms with, too. Soon after I joined the family, one of the children was very distressed by a series of nightmares about witches. We told her that there are no such things as real witches, but that sometimes real things that frighten us appear in dreams as witches or monsters. The child's face lit up and her whole body relaxed as she said, 'Oh, I dream about you and you turn into a witch !'

In the stories, the children sorrowfully accept the cruel circumstances in which they are placed by the wicked step-parent. Then agents for good come to their rescue - a Fairy Godmother, perhaps. Is this an expression of longing, of wishful thinking: or another view of grace?

My new attitude to responsibility and guilt has various results which I am just beginning to see. If guilt for past misdeeds is no longer necessary, then punishment for the past is irrelevant, and so is reward. So I can begin to shed, for myself, the unconstructive resentments that go with the view, 'That's not fair.' And if punishment and reward, and fairness, are irrelevant to me, then they are, perhaps, irrelevant to others. That carries all sorts of implications for all sorts of people: teachers, parents, those dealings with offenders against the law.

Another result is that I now feel in a curious way privileged to be in touch in a small measure with the darker sides of other people's lives. For example, it is easy to say, 'How can those people in Northern Ireland do such terrible things?' But I know that I have in me the seeds of just such violence. I also know the grace of a new beginning, and I know that I hold in me the seeds of love and hope. And all territories, and all step-parents, and all people, hold in themselves, as well as the seeds of violence, the seeds of love.

MARGARET FAWCETT

first published in *The Friend*, 16th November 1979

Facing Sexual Abuse

I was washing up the supper dishes on Sunday evening when I heard my daughter talking to her friend on the telephone in the next room and it became clear to me that she had been sexually assaulted by the leader of a play-scheme where she had been working as a volunteer. It is hard to describe the shock. I am a social worker and had dealt with sexual abuse many times but it had never occurred to me that it might happen to my child. In the weeks to come that was to weigh heavily with me for I felt that I could have done so much more to prepare her for, and to help prevent, such an eventuality.

Although I had talked to her about protecting herself from strangers, I had never talked to her about the dangers from people she knew and trusted. It is sad that we should have to do this and yet the statistics show that children are far more likely to be abused by people they know than by strangers.

I did not speak to Anna about what I had overheard as we needed time to decide what to do. Thus there began a period of nightmarish unreality, behaving as normal, and yet fearing that once this came out into the open things would never be the same again. How would Anna react to my eavesdropping on her conversation? If we took any action would she ever forgive us? We did not know what to do. Our instincts were against involving the police; we had always held to the Quaker belief that one should only go to law as a last resort. Yet even at that stage we could see that without police intervention we might not be able to stop it continuing. Furthermore the man concerned had access to a number of vulnerable young people.

One of the problems for me was that I knew him quite well: he was one of life's unfortunates, inadequates, keen to please, somehow sad. He had obtained his post after a period of unemployment and seemed to be doing it well. He was in his forties, lived alone and seemed isolated. Yet I realised that, despite all that, he had to be responsible for his own actions.

Another problem was the fear that it might not have happened. Teenagers are funny creatures - maybe it was a fantasy - maybe Anna had been trying to impress her friend. How awful it would be if I blundered in and trampled on her awakening fantasies. Worse still, maybe I had misheard or misinterpreted what she had said. The next day I discussed it with a social work colleague and came to see that I had no alternative but to inform the police.

Once the police were informed I lost any control over what happened, but they did allow me time to talk to Anna and explain to her why I had had to report it. That was one of the most painful things I have had to do as a parent. I cannot speak too highly of the skill and patience of the policewoman concerned (from the Woman's Specialist Unit) nor of the social worker who shared the interview and did some ongoing work with Anna. The finished statement was full of pathos: a young teenager with all the awakening sensations of woman-hood trying to cope with the bewildering mixture of fear, anxiety, excitement and secrecy - and all spelt out in short inadequate sentences so that it read like a school exercise.

The man was questioned subsequently and admitted the offence. I shall always be grateful to him for that, for it meant that Anna did not have to appear in court. Even more importantly, it meant that all the doubts had disappeared. We knew exactly what had happened and we could begin to cope with it.

I was quite surprised by Anna's reaction. Her overriding emotion seemed to be of immense relief once it was out. I think the secrecy had become an intolerable burden, and I have often wondered if I was meant to hear the telephone conversation. There is no doubt that she had been very attached to this man. I had felt it to be her first teenage crush and had watched it with amused interest. It had felt so natural. What was not natural, of course, was the man's response to her interest. Instead of treating that in an adult fashion he had used and abused her affection to satisfy his own needs. How foolish I had been to assume that because he was past forty he would behave as an adult.

What became apparent from her statement and her sub-sequent behaviour was that he had managed to kill her love. Once she was relieved of the burden of secrecy and intrigue she had no further feelings for him. She did not appear to grieve at the loss of his friendship. In fact the only outward sign of inner turmoil was the fact that she refused to wear ever again the jumper that she had on when the police came.

It is too early to know if there has been lasting damage. Such an awful betrayal of trust and the brutal ending of her first love affair may have left its mark and make it difficult for her to make a satisfying and adult relationship with a man. Only time will tell. Immediately after her interview with the police Anna started working with her social worker. This focussed on the whole subject of relationships - seeing them as positive and something to which she could look forward, but at the same time learning to say 'no' to demands that are inappropriate. She chose her own time to bring this work to a close.

As far as the man is concerned, he was given a large fine. This felt inappropriate. I had hoped that he would be placed on probation so that he could share some of his problems, and hopefully prevent a repetition. He lost his job. I have had to work very hard not to feel guilty about him, and I still feel extremely sad. The loss of his job was a bitter blow and for a long time I felt as though Anna and I had been responsible. I wondered whether I should have gone to the police or whether there might have been some other way that we could have ended the affair. Yet I do know that people involved in sexual abuse tend to be devious and that any informal agreements we may have made could have been circumvented by him.

Without watching Anna every moment of the day we could not have been sure that they were not meeting, and that would have been an infringement of her liberty at a time when she was needing to grow and develop and learn to use independence. At the end of the day it is the responsibility of adults to control their sexual desires, and everyone shares the responsibility to protect vulnerable youngsters. Both the policewoman and the social worker were extremely helpful both with Anna and myself by talking about our feelings of guilt.

After it was all over I began to think carefully about prevention and contacted the Children's Resources Room at Friends' House to see what material they had. I found that there was a wealth available in the form of books, both for parents and for children themselves. I borrowed these from my local library. There are several easily read books designed in story form for children, which advise them that if they are unhappy about the way they are being touched to confide in a 'safe' adult (sadly it cannot always be the parent as so often a parent is the abuser). I felt these books would have been extremely helpful to Anna had she had access to them, and I would like to see them available to all children in the pre-teen age group.

To my horror I found that none of these books were on the library shelves as they were marked 'for reference only' and were kept at Headquarters. It is hard to imagine an anxious sexually abused child going to the reference library at Headquarters to do their research! I wrote to the County Librarian and since then those books have been freely available in this county. I feel that in this way some good may have come out of Anna's sad experiences.

None of us likes to think about sexual abuse and when we are forced to do so we look upon it as something which happens to other people. We cannot afford to be so complacent. The long term damage to young people who are sexually abused is immeasurable, and we should never underestimate the seriousness of it. Not only do they suffer physically and mentally as children but their ability to make long term adult relationships can be impaired permanently. Those of us who are parents have a special duty, but all of us who come into contact with children and adolescents need to follow the advice of *Questions and Counsel* and...

'watch tenderly over the children who are in trust to us from God.'

ANONYMOUS

Extracts from
A Welcome Letter

Dearest Rachel Ann

Welcome, daughter, to our family! You don't know how long I have waited and hoped for a little girl of my own to love! I am deeply thankful to God for sending you swiftly and safely to me, and for helping to make you so big and beautiful.

When your brother came to visit, I received a large, quick dose of reality, and almost began to wish that this time for us would just go on forever. You were my lifeline to happiness and normality. But how guilty I felt for these feelings, for I love your father and your brother so much and want, in the end, for us all to be happy together.

Your brother was born with a problem that would have killed him immediately were it not for a serious operation. He had many other problems resulting from that operation and a long period of hospitalization. Your daddy and I couldn't even hold him until he was two months old, and he couldn't come home to live with us until he was almost six months! You see why our time in the hospital was so precious to me. I never had that with Jonathon. When you are old enough to understand it all, we will tell you about the extraordinary efforts to save his life. And when you are older you will notice that your friends' 'normal' lives seem much happier and easier than your own (whether or not they really are).

Most of the time we can go about living happily and being so proud of Jonathon and all that he has learned to do. He is so cheerful and loving. We love him very, very much and are glad he is part of our family. You will learn to love him too.

But there will be times when you don't feel loving towards him. You will have some terrible feelings that will scare you and make you feel ashamed. All siblings have bad feelings toward each other sometimes, but you will have more because of Jonathon's problems. I know because I had some scary and shameful feelings growing up with your Grampy who was physically impaired, often in much pain, and whom I loved very much. I knew he couldn't help the way he was, and he was awfully smart and brave and capable, but it made our lives so complicated and so different.

I watched my friends play with their fathers and hug their fathers and jump in the car and go somewhere with their families without having to gather a trunkful of special equipment and a bag of medicine first. And when they reached their destination they didn't have to send somebody ahead to reserve a particular table or find wheelchair access or carry the chair cushions. They could run right in and get settled. I always wished things could be that simple for my family. It is similar with Jonathon, both the inconvenience and the bad feelings.

Please know that these feelings are okay and they don't make you a bad person. It's okay for you to feel angry that Jonathon takes so much of our time with doctor visits and hearing tests and eye tests and therapy sessions, not to mention measuring and administering medicine and filling out forms and making phone calls and spending so much money for special toys and medicine and equipment.

You won't like these feelings in yourself, and you will feel guilty and confused by them as I often do, but try not to. The feelings themselves are normal and I want you to know that I do understand and will be glad to talk to you at any time about these things. The worst thing would be if you felt you had to keep them inside and not let anybody help you with them because you are supposed to be a 'good sister'.

Let me begin to end this letter by saying that one good thing about having Jonathon in our family is that we have learned not to take anything for granted. We appreciate all the little things he is able to do, and your growing (even though we expect it) is very special to us, too. We have learned to be thankful for what gains have been made, as each required so much time and effort from so many. And we are especially thankful that you are so strong and healthy, because we know not all babies are.

Another good thing: you will learn well the lessons of giving and receiving. Some unique gifts I received taught me to be a more helpful and sensitive giver, and I expect that for you it will be the same. Sensitive givers understand that we all need opportunities both to give and to receive.

The challenges you will encounter even in your childhood will be great, and I am truly sorry that I cannot give you an easier place to grow up. But I can assure you, as I have always been assured, of a place in our own and in our extended family where you will be loved and respected and well cared for. In addition you will have an early introduction to the Holy Spirit and the wider family of Friends, both of which will be sources of real strength and comfort.

Loving you so much and wanting to give you a wonderful life.

Your Mommy

KATHRYN E HOOD
first published in *Friendly Woman*, vol.8 no 4

THE FOLLOWING anonymous contribution about feelings of inadequacy, of failure, as a parent was submitted without a title.

I've been feeling a failure as a parent for some years. Our son seems so unhappy, so destructive of self and others, that we must have failed him dreadfully.

We hoped we were teaching our children to love and to be confident of being loved; to have a proper sense of safety along with a joy of life and a sense of purpose. We were quite prepared for our son to leave home, frighten us with dangerous sports, surprise us by his choice of career or partner, political party or church, but, instead, we have seen him steal, hurt his own body, hurt other people and play deadly games with solvents and unprotected sex.

Friends reassure me that he's just going through a phase, that teenagers have to assert their independence, that he'll survive his mistakes and learn from them, but the danger signs seem too serious for such glib optimism.

One tattoo is not uncommon but to go on even after skin infections seems perverse. Again, an earring is quite normal these days, but to have rows of holes in the ears and the nose looks like self-mutilation. He seems reckless about his body - actually we don't know whether he is reckless and uncaring or hates himself, or is trying to show he controls his own life.

We tried to accept all these things as normal teenage behaviour and, indeed, most of his friends in this inner-city area seem much the same. However, there was one occasion when he had to be rushed to hospital with alcoholic poisoning.

He was drinking alone; the note that he left was despairing. This was a terrible grief to us but what shook me was his anger afterwards. He was angry that we'd called the ambulance, angry with the medical staff and angriest with the psychiatrist. He walked out of family therapy and refused to talk with anyone, including me, and I found it very difficult to be tender to him. I don't *want* to be an uncaring parent, nor do I want to fail him if he needs me, but I'm scared to let myself be rejected like that again.

His despair seems to have faded recently only to be replaced by solvent abuse. Finding the lighter fuel in his room helped by explaining his wild moods and violence. We could get no clear guidance from our counsellor on responding to addiction. However, we'd suspected for a long time that he was stealing from us and decided we could not share in the abuse by paying for it in any way. His moods seem a bit calmer now. Maybe our behaving clearly according to our principles was not just right for us but helpful to him.

When I look back over the last few years, I can see he has dropped some activities, so there is some hope. For example, it's over a year since the last tattoo but, on the other hand, he scorns unprotected sex. We are still thinking this one through. He could well be HIV positive already - do we have a responsibility to his partners? Should we keep condoms in the bathroom cupboard beside the shampoo?

Always there are the questions about our function as parents. He should be living independently now and we should be fading into his background, available for love and emergency help. Instead, he has no plans to leave home, insisting on his right to lead his own life without interference yet making it impossible for us to stand by calmly; so often hating us, hating himself and neither working nor studying. It almost feels as if he has chosen to die slowly and it doesn't worry him to see us grieving already.

We were helped by a counsellor in our efforts to understand ourselves and we have had a lot of support from close friends. I have been carried by other's prayers when I have been unable to pray myself and we have had to re-examine our faith over the last few years.

'Walk cheerfully' - but how ? 'Answer that of God in every one' - we'd certainly failed at that ! For about two years I could hardly attend Meeting for Worship but then I realised that these were not commands of George Fox but promises of rewards if we live according to the principles that we know are tried and true. If you do help other people it's not because you've tried and can claim the credit but because God works through you. That relieves me a little of my burden of guilt - humility, letting go, is actually very healing.

I *have* tried looking for that of God in my son and I know it is there, but he sees my clumsy looking as intrusive and manipulative. I can try to be a pattern of steadiness and caring, and being valiant for truth has become particularly important. When our son seems to lose touch with reality it becomes vital that we should be scrupulously factual and truthful.

Our friends don't know how much we feed on their strength, companionship and prayers but I do wish that they would sympathise when I express the little I can without breaking our son's confidence. It's easy to talk about your toddler's sleeplessness and people believe you and listen. It's much more upsetting when you want to talk of your grown-up son's behaviour but cannot say much without betraying him. At this point friends have a tendency to be jolly and bracing which leaves one even more alone. So, thank you, dear reader, for going this far with me, and, next time you meet parents who feel negative, but don't go into much detail, don't dismiss them as fusspots or pessimists. Instead, listen a bit and pray for them. The need might be greater than you can see.

ANONYMOUS

Remember that thou art not more indebted to thy
parents for thy nature, than for their love and care.

WILLIAM PENN
Reflections & Maxims no:177

Forcing Children to Meeting

First day morning started quietly enough. Breakfast was set as usual. Then my twelve year old daughter found the dog had vomited on her bed quilt. Later I yelled at her sister when the dog jumped out of her arms to avoid ear medication. As events unfolded in the final minutes before departure for meeting, she announced she could not get dressed until she had read the newspaper columns which her sister was beginning to read in the corner of the kitchen.

At three minutes to departure, without shoes on, she announced she was not going to meeting, which was her choice according to long-standing family policy. Her sister announced solidarity and invoked the free choice policy. My wife, Joanne, and I left for meeting alone.

My anger at my daughter's refusal to attend meeting was partially due to the circumstances of the morning and the chain of events. These situations occur and take on a quick momentum of their own before the participants are even vaguely aware of their power and their attachment to deeper themes of family life. Life presents these constellations of happenings. They occur all the time. They are part of family life.

But in a larger sense, these events and their effects are a part of the adolescence through which we are all passing - daughters and parents. Despite all the good parenting advice, adolescence is not easy for anyone. And I am not as flexible as I need to be.

I regret and fear losing that control a parent exercises by virtue of strength and knowledge when children are young. While I know adolescence is a period for consistency in guidelines and loosening control with progressive widening of the scope of individual decision making. I feel big parts of this parent are being dragged where other parts want to lead.

At a deeper level, there is a greater obstacle than those brought by adolescence itself. That obstacle is my fear. I fear that, in their new freedom, my daughters will reject that which is important in my life - the life of the spirit of God in Meeting for Worship. Many Quaker parents experience this. It is painful and produces parental self-doubt and self-re-crimination.

This fear is the ground of my anger - and it will be the source of its own fulfilment if I am not careful and sensitive to my actions in this regard. Meeting for Worship is important to me in a life-giving way. Through meeting I touch a source of the holy reservoir of God and become connected with others in this holy circle, in the process of God's acting in the universe. Meeting brings this touch week by week, sustaining and informing my life.

We have worked hard to introduce our daughters to this source, to permit them to taste its depth and richness. This has been a twelve-year old process with the usual ups and downs but without the crisis of refusal. As our daughters grow towards adulthood I must face the test of their free choice. The fear that they will reject what is so central to my life gets in the way. Part of me chooses the present comfort of outward conformity to family ritual and tradition. Their free choice does not seem as important in areas so central to my life.

Looking at this situation from outside, it is a cause for laughter in its irony. My own pilgrimage is the story of free choices and some thwarted family expectations. I prize that free choice for myself but would deny it to those I love the most. Part of me would have their lives in conformity to my choices and without thought for the possible future costs.

I know that parental example is the essential teacher of children in spiritual education. I cannot preach what they can clearly see is not connected to my life. Yet I want it both ways. Their freedom to choose and conformity to my desires. The contradiction looms and can become an impacted and chronic condition which poisons our family system.

As I worked on these thoughts in the river of Light in meeting that morning, realization dawned that this is at the core of our family life. Forcing our daughters to attend meeting would destroy the purpose of attendance. As much as I wanted their attendance, I wanted more their progressive freedom to choose in the spiritual life. Not yet knowing how to break the cycle of refusal and demand but appreciating the new clarity, a piece of grace entered the holy circle.

As with grace in all my life, it came particularly unmerited, free, and uncontrolled. It came from a source beyond my parental authority, my education, my past work, and my efforts.

My daughters slipped into seats in the circle in the waning minutes of meeting. It was a long walk in the bitter November cold to the meeting. The circle glowed in the hand of God.

Whether my daughters will decide in the future that Meeting for Worship is the source for their lives that it is for mine, or whether they go their own ways in their spiritual pilgrimages, I do not know and cannot know. Times will be trying and tempers will rise. Events will chain themselves together and, to our surprise, catch us all up in their links. I will be tempted again to force conformity to meeting attendance as my fears rise again. But now I know in a new way. New light has penetrated the fog. I know again and will remember a bit more of the bittersweet taste of God's grace in the events of my life, sustaining my decisions and actions and enlarging the scope of my understanding.

LAWRENCE J SPEARS
first published in *Friends Journal*, 15.6.85

Teenage Sexuality

As a teacher I have always found it relatively easy to accept the developing sexuality of my pupils, to participate in their personal and social education - explaining the correct way of using a condom, the nature of sexually transmitted diseases, the arguments for and against abortion. I had no difficulty in accepting the fact that a large number of sixteen year olds were sexually active - I feel able to talk and listen to them without embarrassment and without being judgemental.

No wonder parents are so anxious for teachers to 'do' the sex education of their children for them. From any perspective, as a parent, it all looks very different. The idea that your little boy or girl has gone through what seems to be a transmogrification and is now a sexual being in his or her own right is alarming and threatening to parents in all sorts of ways - not least in throwing aspects of their own relationship into sharp and uncomfortable relief.

There is a feeling of unease, uncertainty and - worst of all - a lack of trust. There is a desire to pretend that 'it' is not happening and the 'catch 22' - that asking questions or offering advice suggests that you are suspicious and do not consider them to be either trustworthy or responsible! In their own eyes they are old enough - buying condoms shows just how responsible you are - and of course you've learnt all about it in Personal and Social Education.

In reality it may turn out rather differently. What happens when, in their inexpert hands, the condom splits and your sixteen year old son comes home with the news that his sixteen year old girl friend is pregnant and then breaks down and cries real tears like the child that he still is, sobbing 'But I do love you Mum'.

How do you feel confronted by her parents? Discussing the pros and cons of abortion is very different when it's for real and not an academic exercise in a P.S.E. lesson!

You've certainly got to talk about it all now. How do you feel when you spend a day in the 'Abortion Ward', watching and waiting, seeing your son walk down to the theatre behind the trolley and anxiously watching the door for its return?

'Situation Ethics' is all very interesting unless you happen to be in the 'situation'! P.S.E. is fine so long as it doesn't all get too 'personal'!

And yet the 'experiential' is a very effective, if sometimes painful, way of learning - growth can and does take place in unlikely situations and the real and urgent need for mutual support can deepen family relationships in a lasting way.

All this angst and anguish is not, of course, the whole story. Living with teenagers, watching them and their friends grow into young adults is also an exciting and rewarding experience. I like the openness of their relationships and I am sometimes envious of the uninhibited way in which they express their feelings and emotions. They are interesting and stimulating; most of the time they 'walk cheerfully' and they give a whole new meaning to what might be involved in 'living adventurously!'

ANONYMOUS

Extracts From a Letter

Florence and I have had a family of five children. About twenty-five years ago when we were struggling with poor school reports and the ups and downs of adolescents, 'Home Service Committee' produced a pamphlet, or a slim book, for parents. It was written by Edgar Castle, a previous headmaster of Leighton Park School and it was a help to us.

One passage in his writing remained with us. He said that when anxious parents came to him with problems over their teenage sons, he told them to come back when the young man was thirty and look at the worry again.

How right he proved to be, for us at any rate. One of ours left with a school report which stated he would never have an academic career. He now has an M.Sc. Another leaving with one 'O' level in Art is now a Health and Safety Executive Officer for a large engineering firm. Yet another who spent his school holidays chasing a guinea pig around the garden has just built a ten thousand pound extension for his house.

What a good thing we waited until they were thirty before despair descended!

HUGH CLUNES

Give children a training suitable to their character and, even when old, they will not go back on it.

Proverbs 22:6

When a Marriage Ends

If a marriage begins to go wrong and there are children involved, the couple will often decide to stay together 'for the sake of the children'. The easy assumption can be that, no matter how far the relationship between husband and wife has deteriorated, the nuclear family unit provides a preferable environment for the child/ren.

Parents must consider very carefully before making this decision.

In my years as a teacher of teenage children and, through the shared experience with my son of the end of my first marriage, I have observed the effects that a failing or broken marriage can have on a child's behaviour, work and entire state of mind. The situation has become so common in the school context that in the case of a major deterioration in a child's performance or attitude, discreet enquiries are first made about the parents' relationship and the effect that it may be having. It is my experience that a child can react in exactly the same detrimental way if parents are continuing to live together in an atmosphere of increasing animosity and intolerance as if the parents have recently separated.

Unfortunately marriages will continue to fail, and children will continue to be involved so, for the good of the children, what is best? Should parents stay together or separate?

Of course there is no general rule for all cases; what is good for one will not necessarily apply to another. Possibly the worst thing that parents can do is to try to hide the obvious from their children. If there is any change in their relationship the children will know, no matter how careful are efforts to hide the fact, and trying to keep it from them could damage each parent's relationship with each child. Openness and honesty have to be the keynotes. It can never be easy but the long-term consequences of a serious mistake could be grave.

What is important, then, is that where there are problems, the children are considered and, even, included in discussions. This does not only apply to older children. It is quite remarkable, and a surprise to many people, even parents, how wise and understanding young children can be. To constantly talk to them, sharing what is happening and being open and honest, can provide the reassurance that the child needs, and children need to be constantly reassured that what is happening is not their fault. They have done nothing wrong. It is common for children to blame themselves for the problems between their parents.

If parents do finally decide to go their separate ways there is always going to be a tendency for their children to harbour the hope that they will get together again, no matter how long and complete the separation might be. If the child has any deep-seated feelings of self-guilt concerning the original separation, this hope is going to be so much stronger as a reconciliation would remove the necessity to feel any guilt at all.

Honesty and openness on the part of the parents, although it may be hard at the time, will show that the child is loved by both parents however their feelings for each other might change and whatever ultimately happens to their marriage.

Although it is unlikely that children will remain totally unaffected by either their parents' separation or a disintegrating relationship at home, by showing them at all stages that you are prepared to share your feelings with them, removing any sense of self-recrimination, they will understand and therefore be more likely to cope better with the trauma that you all face.

KEITH REDFERN

The original aim of this anthology was to collect personal experiences from a specifically parenting context and, with the exception of those from Gijubhai, Penn and the Bible, all of the contributions to this point reflect that. We were, however, offered two items which share experiences in which parents have been offered help and support from an external source.

These contributions are included in the hope that they may enable and encourage others to provide similar assistance if a need is seen to exist.

Meetings for Parents
Cheshire Monthly Meeting

Two years ago, following a Preparative Meeting weekend at Glenthorne Guest House, Grasmere, it occurred to me that a number of parents in the Monthly Meeting could do with some support. I wrote a letter to my PM Overseers to see if I was thinking rightly and to see if they thought the same. My letter was passed to Monthly Meeting and the need for provision of some sort of support for parents was discussed there. I was encouraged to set up occasional gatherings for parents in the Monthly Meeting.

All parents were written to personally to invite them to a meeting and Overseers were asked to check in their local Meetings that those Friends who wanted to attend had babysitting or transport problems overcome.

Twenty-four parents attended the first meeting at which three people spoke briefly about their family life and a general discussion ensued. Time for informal chat and refreshments was allowed. We agreed to meet further.

Though numbers have dwindled a little we have had good sessions. One on *Christian Faith & Practice* §436-499, another 'sharing' on family life, an evening ramble and supper at a Friend's home and an evening of craft activities.

We continue to notify all parents by letter of gatherings arranged and we hope to look at the subjects of being a single parent and drug and alcohol abuse in the future and perhaps have another ramble in the summer.

We have moved around the Meeting Houses in the Monthly Meeting in order to make it easier for people to attend.

JULIET BATTEN

The Life of a Mothers' Group

It seemed to me that the playgroup which my daughter attended at our local community centre was tarnished with a general inertia, despondency and lack of confidence about parenting and the understanding of children's needs. Many parents seemed to lack self-esteem and seemed not to have had the opportunity to explore their full potential as women. I felt that the playgroup lacked a heart and a soul: there seemed to be no true sense of community generated by the parents and the staff. I felt confident that if a solid core group could be created, that valued itself and felt cared for and nourished, individuals might realise their potential and the group might help to generate a sense of community, wholeness and an understanding of the children's needs. With this in mind I proposed the idea of a Mothers' Group to the centre co-ordinator, who responded by securing funding for me from an Adult Education budget.

I have a holistic vision of life, recognising the intrinsic value of individuals as part of a whole ecological system and that 'the truth' or 'answers' for each one of us lie within ourselves. For this reason I chose to run a Mothers' Group where individuals would be free to explore their own solutions to issues they raised. I would provide the framework to enable this to happen and would receive support from my supervisor. It was decided that the Mothers' Group would run once a week for an hour. I would have the use of the same room each week and would provide tea, coffee and a crêche. I determined to keep the mothers who attended the group in touch constantly by writing to them when they missed a session, so that they would know that we were still thinking about them. In this way I hoped to ensure the development of the group as of a living organism. I would be mother to the Mothers' Group. I was aware that most mothers enjoy being mothered and that some potential participants might have had poor or indifferent experiences of mothering and might come to value a time for themselves.

The group began one misty, December morning. It was a tentative, unspectacular beginning. Eight women appeared and we sat around drinking tea and coffee whilst we talked of what the group might be and about childbirth experiences - an appropriate topic for the start of a group. Over the weeks that followed a variety of topics emerged. There was, predictably, much concern about confidentiality, trust and safety. Mothers were exploring the possibilities of the group and were testing it out to see if it was a safe place to bring worries and concerns.

We talked of the suitability of the crêche, our children, our separation from them and the rôle of mothers, this latter topic seemed to be clearly linked to whether or not I could be trusted to run the group. One week I sat for an hour alone in the room. This felt like a challenge to my rôle as facilitator. Would the group continue if it were rejected by its members? The following week five mothers appeared again and we re-established ourselves!

Gradually greater trust began to emerge as it became clear how much the group could withstand and that it was not about to disappear. One woman was experiencing a divorce and so we were able to support her. This led us to think about relationships with partners and children.

The issue of smacking was broached and what constituted the abuse of children - indeed what abuse were women prepared to tolerate themselves? One woman brought an incidence of sexual abuse to the group. This raised issues for everyone and we wondered about our roles when such a confidence was divulged. We encouraged her to seek the help that she needed.

There was much debate about the roles of women at home, at work and within society. Many women were beginning to believe that they had a right to lives beyond their homes alongside their roles as wives and mothers. We invited people to talk about women's health issues, education and training opportunities and we talked about dealing with those in authority, particularly in relation to the benefits that some women struggled to claim.

Women also began to share their own skills of cookery, sewing and embroidery and asked me to run a session on child development. They began to help more in the playground and two women began to run the Centre's Mother and Toddler Group and set up a Weight Watcher's Group. A Friday Lunch Club also evolved.

Eventually my own rôle within the group was challenged. Questions were again asked about what the group was for and attendance became erratic. One morning I arrived to find everyone there already, busily making Easter bonnets for the playgroup. They were telling me that they didn't need me in the same way anymore. The group was growing up!

On reflection I realised that individual women had also changed. One woman who had come to the group traumatised after childbirth had shared her experiences of early motherhood and had begun to own her own authority. Another who had had three children in quick succession had had particular difficulties with her eldest son. Their relationship had improved as had her relationship with her husband. Another had been particularly negative about herself and others and lacking in self-esteem. Her poor relationship with her daughter had begun to improve and, now divorced, she wanted to begin a painting and decorating course.

Soon after the Easter bonnet incident and eighteen months after the beginning of the group, my family's plans to move away were confirmed. This seemed appropriate timing as I felt that even if my rôle were not replaced the group could now sustain itself. There was still time for a requested event on multi-cultural issues to be organised, for the future planning of the group and for issues about leaving to be considered.

I shared my mixed feelings about leaving the group, London and moving to Wales. This enabled members to share feelings about losses they had experienced and to anticipate the group without me.

As this point spirituality was also raised as a topic. The group shared their different ideas about faith and the importance of accepting a God in their lives. What impressed me was the group members' ability to listen and to accept one another's differences. We also spent a session talking about food. Who would feed whom in the future, I wondered?

A goodbye party was arranged for me after the last session. This session felt particularly messy with lots of coming and going and a feeling of restlessness. Endings are often like that. One year later I heard that the group was still meeting, members supporting one another without the help of a paid worker.

Told like this the group sounds ordered and well shaped. There were, however, struggles encountered which needed constant attention and vigilance. For instance, my relationship with the centre staff and crêche workers needed constant nurturing to maintain an effective working environment.

On reflection, I feel that the group met the needs of the centre at a time when it was needing sustenance and support for its playgroup. It also supported individual women at times of change and encouraged them to find their own answers to issues of concern and to develop their self-esteem. The group developed its own creative life, a source of energy greater than its individual parts which empowered women to rise above their particular oppression and to realise more of their potential and worth.

JENNY JONES

Afterword

A friend of mine has a theory that the main difference between children and adults is their concept of time. I can remember my brother in answer to my mother's 'I'll do it in a minute' saying, 'Do you mean a grown-up minute or a children's minute?' He was beginning to appreciate the difference.

'Always remember that the most important thing you can give your child is time'. This was the advice given to a soon-to-be-mother by her mother. This Friend writes: 'She spoke words of wisdom' but faces the 'battle between being involved in all the good causes that I feel are worthy of my time and effort, whilst at the same time giving my children the time that they so need and that I feel is so important.'

Books and articles I have read talk about 'quality' time not 'quantity' time. The value of even fifteen minutes spent with one of our children when they have our total attention must be more valuable than a lengthier time when, although we may be in the same place, the adults attention is concentrated on numerous other things and the child gets the occasional 'crumb'.

When our children are small the time spent pacing the floor with a sleepless baby or walking to and from the school gates seems to fill our lives and be never-ending but looking back, once the children have grown and left home, these childhood years seem to have vanished in a flash.

One of the hardest lessons I learnt was when my son was three. Two small boys from his playgroup were run over and killed one Saturday morning as they played on their front lawn. The fragility of my own child's life was brought home to me very strongly - and I vowed never to put off his requests by saying, 'not now, I'm busy'. By the time I had stopped being busy it might be too late.

For most of our years as parents we juggle with the various calls upon our time, our jobs, our interests, our children, our partners and all the attendant tasks necessary to maintain life in a reasonable order. The decisions as to how we prioritise our time are subject to all sorts of outside pressures often beyond our control. Small wonder that we often feel depressed, angry, confused, and a failure.

Now I am an 'empty-nester' (as the insurance agent so graphically described me) there are things, of course, that I wish had happened differently. But looking at the 'end result' I must have done some things right!

SUE COLLINS

Index

Index

Index